# LITTLE WORLDS OF MAGIC

*Mysteries are everywhere*
*Mary T Kincaid*

## MARY T KINCAID

### Illustrated by Doriano Strologo

REDHAWK PRESS

Text Copyright © 2016 Mary T Kincaid
Illustrations copyright © 2016 Doriano Strologo
Cover Image by Doriano Strologo
All rights reserved.
ISBN-13: 978-0997148800
ISBN-10: 0997144802

# DEDICATION

For everyone trying to fit in.

# ONE

**August 1**

I spent the afternoon drifting on the horizon hunting like a hawk for my next wave to ride. I glided along, one with the ocean, the sun, and the water. I thought my life should always be like this. Why not? It'd been my life as long as I could remember. But now I'm home sitting at the dinner table with the Commander, my father, and my mother.

The Commander's announcement of "We're moving" brought my world to an end. "We're transferred to Blytheville, Illinois, for the Great Lakes Navel Warfare Planning and Strategy Center."

I held my breath. I watched his mouth move.

"What...what'd you say?" I asked when my breathing was normal. My checks felt hot.

."We're moving," the Commander restated. He looked me in the eye.

"No, it's not true," I shouted turning to my mom for verification.

"Yes, Mason," she said. "I'm sorry. You'll be too far from the lake to surf. We'll explore other things you can do. This is hard because our moves never affected you before."

"Surfing is the only thing I can do," I said too angry to think about alternatives.

"It's time to explore other things," the Commander said. "You can't surf forever. We'll live some place new, some place different, and you'll adjust like every other person who moves."

I jumped from the table and ran to my room. Tears ran down my cheeks, and nothing I could do stopped them. I threw myself on my bed and fell asleep. I dreamed I was trying to surf on a fresh water pond. I know it can be done, but it can't be the same as the ocean. I dreamed my new friends were scaly blue-green foul smelling monsters reaching up from the pond bottom tipping my board. I awoke in a sweat. I threw off my covers, and lay there with new tears wetting my pillow. Frisbee, my feline brother, came over and licked my face dry. I've surfed since I could hold onto a board. My father taught me and carried me out on his board as soon as I could swim. We rode the waves together at Coronado Beach. The Commander, who hadn't surfed with me in awhile, went to sea for the Navy. I've spent the last three summers on the beach with my boogie board taking lessons: learning about swells, currents, and riding the waves. My surfing friends are the only ones I have. What will I do when I don't have surfing?

**August 15**

I sat on the steps and watched the moving van leave San Diego. This was really happening. I picked up Frisbee's cat carrier and crawled into the back seat of our van. I settled the cat carrier in the center of the floor behind the front seat where Frisbee likes to ride. I looked up at my old bedroom window as we pulled away.

"Okay," I whispered to Frisbee. "We're going on a new adventure. Ready or not...."

# TWO

**August 20**

I walked into the kitchen where mom was scrubbing. Everything smelled like lemon cleaner. She was scrubbing the cabinets and unpacking the boxes of dishes.

"How was your first night in your new room?" Mom asked.

She handed me a bowl, a spoon, and a carton of milk. Packing material and boxes were everywhere. She rustled paper, pulling glasses out of the box in front of her.

"It was okay," I said. "I hate moving. It's so hard. Why couldn't Dad be an electrician? I don't have my friends or my stuff."

I filled my cereal bowl and watched my milk turn pink from the Cherry O's. I picked up my spoon. My mom hugged me. Outside I heard the wind in the trees.

"I know it's hard leaving Bryan, Dylan, and Coronado Beach. You'll make new friends. You'll find new things to do, things you'll like as much as surfing. I think your games and other stuff are in boxes in the basement," Mom answered. "I'll look for them later. Why don't you explore the neighborhood while I get these kitchen boxes unpacked, and into an orderly cabinet?"

Just then, my dad entered the kitchen wearing his khaki uniform ready for work. "You'll have to be the leader when making friends, Mason. You can approach people first. You're not shy. You want me to look for Explorer Clubs? Think about other things you'd like to do."

"Yes, see if you can find a club. I like orienteering, it's fun," I answered moving toward the door.

"It's a good way to meet people," my dad said sipping his coffee cup.

I walked into the yard. I spun in a slow circle looking at everything around me. In the front yard, there was an ancient tree that extended one of its branches toward my bedroom window. Its finger leaves touched the glass. Trees hung over the street making a green tunnel, my sidewalk ran down the block next to the street. I walked along the sidewalk looking around. I didn't see anyone and wondered if everyone was working. Where are the people my age? In the next block, I found a small park. I'd never lived close to a neighborhood park. The entrance rose as an old wooden bridge passed over a giant culvert. A stream trickled down rocks cascading from one side of the culvert, and pooled with other waters in a pond at the center. On the other side of the entrance, a giant rose bush arched. From the sidewalk, the bush looked like it had dark eyes, and a mouth. *Oh wow, a spooky entrance.*

The park was scooped like a bowl with high sides. Along the sides were a line of old trees. A strange smell made my eyes water as I continued along the sidewalk. The trees shaded most of the paths, and formed a high ceiling. Down from the heavens a single shaft of light fell onto the narrow strip of sand meeting the water's edge. It was as if the center of the place was under a microscope.

In the spot of light, a red haired boy danced. He had his ear buds plugged in. His arms wind-milled around while his legs pumped up and down at the knees. He was jamming away. On one of his circles, he caught a glimpse of me and stopped dancing.

"Oh, hello," he said. "What's your name? My name is Ted Brown."

"Hi, I'm Mason Garcia," I said.

"You're with the new family. I saw the moving van yesterday. I live in the next block," he said. He pulled the ear buds out and turned off his tunes.

"Yes," I said. "Do you spend much time here? This park is something," I looked around me.

"I stay here as much as I can," he said. "I love to dance on the beach to my music. No one criticizes me or tells me to stop thumping."

"I see why you like it. It's like having an outdoor room. I've never seen any place like it. It looks ancient," I said.

"It's my secret place. Not many people come here. I guess our neighbors are too busy. None of my brothers care about it, but now you know my secret," Ted said.

"The pond here is not the ocean, not even a little. Even smells different. I miss the ocean," I said. "My dad is in the Navy, that's why we moved here, his new job." I sat down on a rock that marked the difference between the grass and the beach. Ted came over and sat beside me.

"The pond is not the ocean, not even close to it," Ted said looking at it. "I've never seen the ocean. Must be big, huh?"

"It's big. I'm going to go. I've got to unpack," I said. "My games and stuff are still in boxes."

"I like to stay out of the house. Do you have any brother or sisters?" Ted asked.

"No, I'm the only one. If I find my Zooman comics, want me to bring you one? See you later." I started back to the house.

"Hope you do," Ted called. "Later."

"What did you find? Tell me all about the neighborhood," Mom said when I entered the kitchen. She was busy stacking dishes in the cabinets.

"It's different here. Not like San Diego at all. I miss the smell of the ocean."

"Well, what does our new place smell like?" Mom asked. "Is it pleasant or does it stink?"

"Smells strong at the park. Like the bug spray dad uses."

"Stinks. Will we get used to it?" she asked.

"Hope so," I answered. "It's a strange smell."

"Strange smell, what else," Mom said.

"I found a really spooky park," I said pouring some juice and sitting on a stool.

"Go on," Mom said.

"It felt haunted," I said. "Maybe it has secrets."

"A park… secrets," Mom muttered. She stuffed the packing into trash bags and tied them at the top. "Put these in the cans."

I walked over and picked up the bags and headed for the door. "I met a neighborhood kid, Ted. Maybe we can be friends."

"Good," Mom said. "That's a start."

I trudged upstairs with my boxes stacking them next to the door while I set up my gaming equipment. I stored our surfing equipment for the future. Maybe our next move would take us back to the ocean. At least that was my hope. Unpacking my comics allowed me to read my favorites again. I found a shelf and put them in order. My inventory of *Zooman*, *The Microbe*, and *Beetle and Lil Dude* was complete.

I set up my game system, and shelved the games. I lugged the ergonomic chair mom gave me to ward off spine deformities upstairs. Last I hung my marine posters: whales, and jellyfish.

I sat in my chair holding Frisbee admiring my work. I loved my old gray cat. W'd been together since we were both babies. He was my confidant and buddy.

"I've got my room the way I want it," I called to Mom.

"Good job," Mom answered.

## THREE

This morning my mom and I went to the school to enroll. I was assigned to Ms. Rainy's fourth grade class with Ted.

"Come to my house this afternoon. It's all right with my mom. I found my comics. Maybe I have *Zooman* you haven't read."

"Just a minute." Ted brought his mother over to meet us.

"This is my mom, Mrs. Lilly Brown. This is Mason and his mother."

Our mothers exchanged phone numbers and friendly words. They agreed that Ted could come over after lunch. Mom and I left school, ran the rest of our errands, and returned home. About one the doorbell rang, I ran to get it.

"Here are the *Zooman*," I said, pointing to the stack that I separated on the bed. "This is Frisbee lifting him off the comics. I'm not really an only child."

"Unless Frisbee teases you, you're an only child," Ted said. "Consider yourself lucky."

Ted read my comics, and I played games. We sat in silence as Ted turned the pages.

"You don't have tunes?" Ted asked, looking around the room.

"No, I don't," I admitted. "I spent so much time on the water that I haven't decided what I like. My father likes marching band music. My mother likes Broadway show tunes. Maybe you could show me what's good?"

Ted's eyes lit up. "Can I ever. I have a lot on my player. Some of it my brother introduced me to, and some of it I found on my own. We'll experiment."

"That'd be great," I said, wondering what kind of music I did like. Dad's music wasn't too bad, and mom's was tolerable, but I wanted my own. Ted was my first friend. My new friend was a red haired boy with freckles, a music nerd. His only outside activity was dancing in a sunbeam. He was not like my surfing buddies. They lived ready to be outside and always up for the next wave. I missed them, the saltwater, and the sun.

In San Diego, my friends and I discussed surfing while we rode to school. I watched competitive surfing where older boys did their stunts. Now I stood at the bus stop watching as the younger kids milled around. I haven't been in the sun all week, My Go Navy backpack stood out like a geek's in this group of Bug-man and Big Kitties. Ted had a brightly colored Acrobat-Man backpack. I watched him as he ran to the bus from his house. His backpack fell from his shoulder while his elbows winged out holding it on his arm. His gray sweater was in his teeth, and his right hand held his breakfast sandwich. The bus driver waited for him. He climbed on the bus with the finesse of a rhino and blundered into a seat near the front. I wondered about Ted being disorganized. The Commander insisted I get up at 0630 so I would be organized for my day. He would ground me for a week if I ran to catch the bus with my breakfast. Before I left the house, I made my bed, organized my room, and ate my breakfast. Chaos was forbidden in my house.

## FOUR

"Daydreaming instead of doing my homework I noticed a branch of the walnut tree just outside my window. The chemical smell drifted through the open window, made my eyes water, and sent me on an internet search."

"Look," I said to Frisbee, who climbed on my desk to join me. "The internet says the smell is caused by the nuts ripening." Frisbee sat politely on the edge of my desk, and moved to settle on my math book while I read to him. He curled up and purred.

"I didn't know walnuts started out green," I continued. Frisbee purred his agreement. Stroking Frisbee, I was sleepy. I needed to focus on my math homework, but a strong desire to put my head down overcame me. I raised my head and rubbed my eyes, trying to focus. I squinted at the cluster of nuts in front of me, then at my math book with Frisbee on it. I looked up at the branch in front of me. I saw a light blink.

"What was that?" I whispered to Frisbee. "Maybe I should wash my face. I saw a tiny green door open in the front walnut. Look, a tiny man closed the walnut door." I continued to study the branch and nuts. "Frisbee, there're more figures gathered on the limb. Look, their faces are dark like the tree branch. Their clothing is green, and they're wearing brown hats. They've boots. They blend with the leaves and stems around the nuts. Am I losing it? Is this new room sending me into a crazy place?" I dropped my head onto my math book, closed my eyes, expecting that when I raised my head they would be gone.

I raised my head and looked at the branch once again focusing on the walnut. I picked Frisbee up and went outside to get a closer look. The man who first stepped through the door had a full gray beard on his brown face and walked a few steps closer to me. He wore a tiny skullcap. I grabbed Frisbee. "Tell me you see them too!" I whispered. Frisbee was starring at the branch in front of us. He made the sound he makes when he is stalking birds. He flicked his tail. "Braghk."

"Okay, good," I said. "You see them, too." I continued to hold Frisbee who was now straining against my hands. He wanted to move to the tree branch, but I stopped him

"Braghk, Braghk," Frisbee continued, crouching down leaning forward ready to pounce.

The tiny men stood and looked back at me. A whisper grew among those beings. It started small and became a distinct hiss.

"Fifteen minutes until lights out, Mason," my mother called from the hall. The beings scattered among the nuts and leaves.

# FIVE

## SEPTEMBER 29

I spent the after school hours playing video games with a frustrated Ted. He'll never be an expert gamer.

"I'm not very good. I'm only on the first level. Where are you?"

"I'm just about to finish level five. What's your character and weapon?"

"I'm the miner. My weapon is the digging ax," Ted answered, holding his controller in his lap.

"No wonder you're at level one, the miner can't do anything but dig. Start another game and choose the explorer, or even the merchant. They get around and do stuff."

We played a little longer, Ted struggling the entire time while I started with another character in Ted's game, and moved to the next level. Finally Ted left for home.

"How was your time with Ted?" Mom asked me after I walked Ted to the door.

"Not good. Ted isn't a gamer," I said. "He is a difficult friend." I hid my face in my hands.

"I even started a new character in his game trying to encourage him. He's not as competitive as Bryan or Dylan. They played for keeps when they played. I guess games are not for everyone."

"Don't give up on the first person you meet here. Everyone is different. You need to appreciate those differences. I'm sure that Ted has a lot to offer as a friend, give him a chance. You'll figure out something you can do together."

The light was fading from my window while I sat down at my desk. I finished playing *Dark Side of Thitheon*.

"Come on, Frisbee," I called to the cat in the doorway. "I'll read the Revolutionary War to you from my history text."

Frisbee jumped to the desk corner, settled himself, and waited politely.

We both looked toward the walnut still hanging on the branch. Another flicker of light, I looked closer. Frisbee stood up and then crouched. The small door opened, and the miniature man stepped out. I blinked and rubbed my eyes. This cannot be happening again.

"Who's there?" I asked, reaching out and taking hold of my cat.

The bearded dark face peeked around the walnut door.

"Do you have special gifts? People can't see us. It's dangerous for us to be seen. We're called pests," the little man said. He stood and studied me. He took a step or two toward me.

"I just moved in. What are you? Are you the only ones?" I asked mystified by the scene in front of me. Frisbee was ready to go, and I knew that he could make the jump from the window ledge to the branch so I held him while he struggled.

"We are Punwees, the Walnut Clan. Punwees are everywhere, but not many people can see us," he continued, studying me while I held the struggling cat. "You are Megatherian."

Two others crept from behind the walnut. The man from the door turned, "this is Ives and Winsor. What is your name?"

"My name is Mason. It would be easier to believe I'm dreaming than to believe that tiny people live in a walnut."

"My name is Tolemar, the Miniscule," the man answered. "You may call me Tol."

"You are not dreaming," Ives continued. "We won't be here any longer. You've seen us and bring us danger. In the summer we live in walnuts."

I noticed the serious expressions on their faces.

"You're leaving because of me? Are you the only ones? Why haven't you been reported and listed on the internet?"

"Yes, we leave," Ives answered. "We cannot stay after we're seen. It is against our laws."

"Where'll you go?" I asked, as Frisbee continued to fight and struggle.

"We'll go to the rocks 'til spring. The walnut tree is our summer breeze home. Winter comes and we go to earth. There're toadstool Punwee clans, rock clans and creek clans. We're everywhere," Tol said.

"How do you get to the rocks?" I asked. "Do you migrate through the house and down the stairs?"

"No," Tol said, he covered his mouth hurumphing. "We sail leaves on the wind currents. We have skills that we get from the earth, and the sky."

"You are tiny things that are everywhere? Nobody ever notices you? Unbelievable," I said, shaking my head. "You've got skills."

"We've lived here for centuries," Tol said, turning to lead Ives and Winsor away.

"Will I ever see you again?" I asked.

"No, never," Tol answered.

"We could be friends," I said. "I could use more friends even if you're tiny."

They disappeared among the nuts and leaves.

I continued to stroke Frisbee trying to calm him.

"What a strange place, Frisbee," I said, turning back to my history text. "Let's go to bed and sleep on this."

I crawled into bed, turned out the lights, and felt Frisbee settle at the foot of the bed.

# SIX

**September 30**

The next afternoon as Ted and I climbed off the bus together, we walked to my house.

"Have you seen anything unusual in your secret place at the park?" I asked him, thinking surely the little people would be found in that spooky place.

"No, just me and the sunbeam, you know it shifts around right?"

"I mean something unusual…."

"Okay, something I've never seen anywhere, anytime. Like flying monkeys? No, nothing flying or hanging out in the trees," Ted said. "You're joking?"

"Have you heard about anything unusual from someone at school?" I asked.

"Like what?" Ted said, stopping in the middle of the street and putting both hands on his hips. "Just spit it out."

"Okay," I said. "I don't want you to make fun of me. Or think I'm crazy."

"I promise," Ted agreed.

By this time we had walked to my porch, and I opened the door and said, "I'll tell you after our snack when we get to my room."

We ate cheese crackers, drank juice, and went to my room.

"Okay," Ted said. "Out with it."

"I saw little people, very tiny even, in my walnut tree last night," I pointed out my window at the tree branch.

"Well, okay," Ted said. "Are they still there? Where exactly?"

"On that tree branch, hmmmm, looks like the walnut has fallen from the tree," I said, standing at the window. "They told me they live all around us. They are called Punwees. The ones I saw were Walnut Clan."

"Is this for real? You're not pulling my leg? I've never heard a report of any tiny people here in town," Ted said. He bent closer to the window and studied the branch. "Do you think everyone can see them?"

"Why not? I've only been here a little while and I saw them."

"Let me see the walnut house. Maybe it'll ring a bell. What if I saw one and didn't know what it was?" Ted said.

"You don't think I'm crazy?" I asked,,, as I turned from the window.

"No," Ted said. "I think you saw something and I want to see it too. I've lived here longer, I deserve to see some special little people."

"I'm going to look out my window tonight. Maybe I'll see something," Ted said. "See you tomorrow. Got to go."

After my chores I searched under the walnut tree. I found several that had tiny doors in them. The Punwee occupants were gone, so I picked them up.

❖❖❖

The next day, standing outside the classroom, Ted brought up the subject.

"Anyone seen little people!" All the faces in the group turned toward him.

"What're you talking about?" Stanley asked.

"I looked last night, and didn't see a thing," Ted said.

"Why would we see little people?" Sam said.

"Mason saw little people," Ted said, turning to me he asked, "Did you bring the walnut house?"

I pulled a walnut out of my pocket. Ted took it. The other boys standing around passed the walnut house among them. Ms. Rainy appeared and stopped beside us, listening.

"What's this?" Ms. Rainy asked. I showed her the walnut house.

"You saw little brown people, the size of grasshoppers, dressed in green, coming out of this walnut while it was hanging on the tree limb outside your window?" Ms. Rainy asked. "I don't know what to say."

"Amazing...isn't it," I agreed, surprised at her reaction.

"I've never seen the walnut houses before."

"Well, come in and take your seat and we'll start class," Ms. Rainy instructed getting right to the day's business. She opened the door and held it while we entered.

Later, standing in the lunch line, Ted called again. "I want to see the walnut house." I took the walnuts from my pockets, and gave them to Ted. Ted tapped Stanley on the shoulder and handed him the walnuts.

"This is the walnut where the Punwees lived. It fell from a tree in Mason's yard. You can barely see the outline of the door, if you look close," Ted said passing the walnuts along the line.

"I looked from my window last night, and I didn't see a thing," Ted said. The walnuts came back to him and he put them on his lunch tray.

"Yes," I added. "The Punwees called me a megatherian. They find a new place to live when they've been seen. They're gone now. Since they're everywhere, I thought maybe one of you had seen one." The boys standing around just shook their heads.

The girls in line in front of Stanley overheard Ted talking to him. They began to giggle and chirp to each other.

"The new boy is seeing little people," Alice sang out.

"Fairies, flying pink ponies will be next, ummmmm. Hee hee," Sylvia added sarcastically.

"Tiny people in walnuts, ha, ha," Maisy chirped. The girls continued to whisper up and down the serving line. Other students snickered and looked at Ted, Stanley, and me.

But the fourth grade boys were more curious. They asked questions. They liked the idea of seeing little people, and they were envious.

"Were they wearing clothes?" Sam called from the back of the line.

"Yes, little clothes, tiny boots," I answered turning around to find the speaker.

"Could I see one?" Stanley asked leaning past the silverware holders.

"You've never seen anything like them before? You'd have to look. I was staring at the branch out my window. I saw them at sunset. Maybe the dim light helps. They're very small. Look all around you. There're many kinds of Punweees-rock, creek, walnut, they might be anywhere."

"I'm going to start looking for them," Stanley called.

"Me, too," other boys exclaimed.

The girls continued to laugh and scoff at them. "Oh brother, little people hunters."

I didn't care if the girls laughed, maybe I'd fit into this strange new place. At least the boys believed me.

❖❖❖

When I walked through the back door, my mom waited for me. She stood by the kitchen counter with my snack.

"Ms. Rainy called me. She is concerned that you're having trouble adjusting to the move. Did you see little people in your room? Why didn't you tell me? We'll get someone for you to talk to. Are you having trouble?"

"Mom, I did see something. I knew that Dad wouldn't believe me. I knew you'd tell Dad if I told you. We're talking about it now, and you don't believe me."

I clenched my fists and said. "Excuse me, I need to be alone." I turned and ran upstairs. "How am I ever going to talk to my parents about the Punwees?" I asked Frisbee when he climbed up on my bed and snuggled beside me.

At dinner my father, The Commander, turned to me and asked, "Did you see anything last night?"

"I saw tiny men come out of a walnut, Dad."

My dad sat there with his Commander's face studying me.

"How is your new school? Are you making friends? Maybe you were dreaming," Dad continued. "I know moving is hard, and I appreciate the sacrifice you and your mother make every time I relocate you. I don't want you to live in the past. I know you were happy in California, but this is today and here we are."

"I saw little people. I talked to them, too. They're gone. I won't see them again," I whispered. We finished dinner in silence.

## SEVEN

My classmates wanted to see the Punwees.

"Mason, help us search," Stanley said to me. "You've seen one and know what to look for."

"Okay," I said. The recess hunts began. I drew a grid of the schoolyard, and we began a search of the grounds. We drew maps and color-coded them. Trees were circled in green, swing poles and playground equipment in blue, and the bushes around the building were brown. Stanley and I became friends. He liked to play video games.

"Where'll we look today?" Stanley asked.

"We looked around this tree and here." I pointed to the grid. I enjoyed being the center of attention, but I expected someone to see one. I didn't expect the hunt to last long.

"Playground is peaceful. I'm proud of everyone," Ms. Rainy said astonished by our new game.

The fourth grade girls watched, but they couldn't be bothered with the hunt. They played their regular games, sang songs, jumped rope, and played four-square. They joked about our attempts to see little beings.

My friends continued their hunts at home, and entered into bragging contests before school each morning. Punwee hunting was our latest adventure.

"Looked between the washer and dryer in my basement," Drew began. "Nothing."

"Looked on the closet floor around my shoes," Stanley said. The boys surrounding us began to laugh. The girls listening giggled.

"Looked hard in the linen closet and nearly fell asleep," James said. "Mom made me go to bed. Nothing moved."

"Winner, James," I called, laughing with the others.

"I can't be the only one who can see them," I said, shaking my head in disbelief. "Isn't possible."

Oliver refused to join in. He had previously been the recess leader. He was disgusted at being ignored while the rest of us hunted. He stepped forward with his hands on his hips. "You attention hog." He said to me stalking away.

❖❖❖

Stanley, a good gamer, rode the bus home with me. He loved to play games, and was a great competitor. After we finished our homework, we defeated villains, and saved kingdoms.

## EIGHT

One afternoon, I sat in my room playing *'Dark Side.'* I was about to fight the big boss, when I heard a voice from the floor.

"Hey, we wanna play."

I looked around wondering who was talking.

"Down here," the voice called again.

"Where are you?" I asked, looking all around.

"Next to the bed leg. Where is your beast?" the voice asked.

"Frisbee is sleeping on the dryer in the basement." I shut the door, sat down on the floor, and looked at the bed leg. A figure dressed in gray climbed down from the dust bunny whirl he was riding. His face was tan and his hair was blond. Two more Punwees stepped out from behind him. They dressed differently than the rider, and they were younger.

"I'm Dubber of the Dust Bunny Punwee Clan." He waved his hand and turned behind him. "This is Radit and Fluw. We want to learn how to play. We've been watching."

"What about the tradition of moving on when humans see you? What happens if your leader finds out you defied tradition?"

"We find out about defying tradition. No one has ever defied tradition before. At least if they have, it has never been recorded in any history that we study. We think that learning to play games will teach us skills that will benefit our society."

"Are you big enough?" I asked looking at their size. "Pushing the keys on the controller is hard."

"We can learn. We're a team. Show us," Dubber said pulling himself up to his full inch and a half height.

"Okay, let's see," I said, putting my hand down for the three of them to step into. I put them on my game console shelf. The monitor tilted down, but the little men could see. Further down on the shelf set my laptop. I pointed. "Here's the controller. Can you do the buttons? See the arrow keys, and other buttons you have to press."

The little guys climbed onto the controller and studied the keys. Dubber stood in the middle between the mushroom shaped keys, Radit moved to the right by the colored buttons, and Fluw moved to the left to the black keys with arrows.

"Show us," Dubber instructed.

"The controller keys move the cursor arrow. You move the arrow and then the game moves. You make your next move here. See if you can move the cursor by jumping on the keys. Start with the colored buttons. Let's see what happens," I said, pointing to the cursor on the screen.

Radit jumped. He jumped again. He looked at the screen and jumped again. They watched the cursor stay put.

"Teach us the way you do it, Mason," Radit said turning to me.

"You mean on the laptop keyboard?" I asked them, scratching my head.

"Yes," Radit said. He marched to the keyboard and jumped on the right arrow key. The cursor moved on the screen. "We can make these keys move. See," he said. "We'll use these keys, forget the controller."

"K… ummmmm," I agreed. "One of you for the up and right keys, and one for the down and left keys, and one to skate across the mouse pad."

"Try it," I said.

"Okay," Dubber said. "We need to practice."

"Let's play a practice game," I suggested. "We'll split the screen and I'll use the controller."

The first game was slow as they worked to get the hang of looking at the screen and moving the arrow.

A sound came from downstairs and startled the Punwees. They froze.

"Oh, that's Mom, it's time for supper. Will you be okay while I'm gone? I'll shut the door so Frisbee won't come in here."

"Okay, good," Dubber said. "We'll get to your beast eventually."

"Leave the computer on," Radit ordered. "We'll play while you're not here and we'll be better next time."

"Okay," I said, getting up.

"Yeah," Dubber called turning toward me as I walked toward the door.

"I turn the computer off when I go to bed," I said, stopping in the doorway and grabbing my doorknob. "My mom always checks on it."

"That's okay," Radit said. "Show us how to turn it on. We'll play tomorrow while you're gone, and we'll be better tomorrow night."

"Can you climb up to the computer?" I asked, wondering about their skills.

"Yes," Dubber said, pulling a tiny grappling hook from his little knapsack. "We climb things."

"Whoa," I said, shaking my head. "You really are everywhere."

"Yes," Fluw said turning his focus back to the screen.

❖❖❖

I went down to supper.

"Busy in your room?" Mom asked me.

"Yes, playing," I answered sitting down.

"Don't forget your homework," Mom said putting the bowl of corn in front of me.

"Yes, I'll get it done," I agreed, spooning one of my favorites, and spearing a pork chop onto my plate.

"How is it going?" the Commander asked coming into the room and pulling out his chair. "Any of the boys at school as active at something as Dylan and Bryan were? They were great athletes. I hope you can make more friends that are active. You need to be interested in some outdoor activity."

I answered, after swallowing the bite of pork chop. "I'm making new friends. They don't seem to have the same sports that I'm used to, not sure I can skateboard after riding the big waves, but maybe a bicycle for getting around."

"Is there anyone you want to have over?" Commander Dad asked me as he filled his plate.

"Not yet," I answered laying my knife down. "Stanley likes video games, and I'm working on making friends."

"Well, let me know," Commander Dad said between bites.

# NINE

**November 2**

I got off the bus, saw a moving truck parked in the driveway of the house across the street, and noticed the realtor's sign was gone.

"Look," I said, pointing to the moving truck.

"Awesome," Ted agreed. "Got to go home. See if you can find out who it is." He walked quickly away from me.

I walked through my yard, and looked over my shoulder as I moved along.

A dusty colored mop of a dog ran from the house with a girl chasing it. The girl's long blond braid fell over her shoulders as she smiled at me. She bent down and picked up the dog. I reached the front step and sat down

"Hi," I said, sitting there wondering what I could say to the creature beaming a smile to make her stay and talk to me. She walked over to me holding the dog.

"I'm Angela, this is Spooky. Spooky because he moves quietly and sneaks. What's your name?" She sat down beside me. "Wanna pet 'em?" She thrust Spooky at me without waiting for my reply.

"I'm Mason," I said stroking Spooky while he licked my face.

"Where do you go to school?" she asked. "What grade are you in?"

"I'm in the fourth grade, Ms. Rainy's class. What grade are you in?"

"In fourth, we'll see tomorrow," she said.

"Maybe you'll get her. Ted lives down the street, and he's in Ms. Rainy's, too." I was desperate to keep her talking. "Do you play video games?"

"Yes, I'm on ninth level of *Aria Kingdoms*. Do you play *Aria*? Save the girl and the kingdom so she can be a princess," Angela said studying me.

"I play everything. I've been playing *Dark Side of Titheon*. Have you played it?" I asked still petting Spooky while he wiggled on my lap.

"Yes, I beat the game last December. It was great but once you beat it, it's boring fast," Angela said.

I know my eyes expressed my surprise as I studied her.

"You've beaten the *Dark*? Maybe we could play." I said.

"The game's fun. We'll play. Got to go." She took Spooky and started across the street. I got up and went inside.

"I see you've met Angela," my mom said to me. "Maybe you can be friends with her."

❖❖❖

The next morning at breakfast my Commander Dad looked up from his oatmeal and said to me, "I see you're hanging out with Ted and Stanley. Mom tells me there's a new girl across the street. You can make her your friend. Friends are people in the real world."

❖❖❖

Angela joined Ms. Rainy's class. She came to play games with Stanley and me. Ted joined us sometimes. Everyone brought their favorite games and controllers.

One afternoon while the three of us were playing, Ted stood and announced, "I still want to see a Punwee." He looked out the window.

"What's a Punwee?" Angela asked. "I heard the girls laughing at school."

"Mason saw a tiny person, right here, through this window," Ted said to her. "He told me and showed me their walnut house."

"We've been looking for them at school and home since," Stanley said.

"Really?" Angela said staring into my eyes as if she could detect the truth.

"Yes. No one else has seen one," I said.

"I'm beginning to think you made them up," Stanley said getting ahead of Angela as they played.

"Have any girls seen one?" Angela asked me.

"No," I answered. "But the girls aren't that interested."

'Ummmm," Angela said. "Weird."

"If you can see them, I can see them," Ted taunted me turning and staring at me.

"That's how I feel," Stanley said over his shoulder.

"Maybe you'll never see one. Don't know why I did," I said. "Let's play *Killer Androids*.

❖❖❖

One afternoon after everyone left, Ted said to me. "You spend more time with them than with me. When you're with them, you ignore me while you're playing."

"I'm sorry, didn't realize," I said.

That night at supper, I asked Dad. "How do you spend time with three friends if one of them is not as good at something as the others?"

"You have to spend time alone with each one of them. You have to be loyal and considerate of their feelings."

Angela and Stanley beat Ted at everything." "She can beat me, too. I don't care. She makes me a better player, but Ted doesn't feel that way."

"Ted has to learn at his own rate," my dad said. "Can you help him get better?"

"I can try. He doesn't have the flair. Games make him mad," I said my chin in my hand.

"What does Ted like to do?" my dad asked me. "Maybe you could do something different together without hurting anyone's feelings."

"He likes to read my Zooman comics, float boats in the park pond, and dance to his tunes. It's too cold to be in the water, but I could think about music. He promised to help me decide what kind of music I like."

"Give it some thought. I bet you can come up with something," my dad said. "I bet you can."

"Okay," I said picking up my plate and heading for the kitchen.

# TEN

## January 15

The Punwee trio worked hard to improve their skills on the keyboard. Soon they were playing at my level, they'd wait under the bed until everyone left then stick their heads out ready to play.

"Man...Ted is so whiny," Dubber said. "Angela is a babe. Stanley is good."

"Can we play with her?" Radit asked, turning to me with his quizzical face.

"Don't you think it'll be creepy if she can't see you. She might think my room is haunted. She might never come back."

The trio bowed their heads in thought, whispering together.

"Let's stand by the keyboard tomorrow and see if Angela can see us," Dubber suggested.

"Okay, if she can't see you, you can't move the keys, or say anything. You'll scare her."

"Got it," the Punwees said holding their thumbs up like I taught them.

❖❖❖

The next afternoon after Ted left, the Punwees crept from behind the back of the laptop and stood right in front of Angela. Dubber was dying to be seen, he waved his arms and jumped around. Angela kept playing. I paused my game and sat beside her. I shook my head at Dubber when she wasn't looking. Angela got up, gathered her things, and said, "See you tomorrow at the bus stop."

I came back to the room after walking her to the door.

"Sorry guys. What if I explain who you are? You can talk to her and play with her. We can't frighten her. Do you want to try tomorrow?"

"It's better than nothing, but we wanted the babe to see us," Fluw said. "Besides she's a better player than you are."

"I know she is. Don't rub it in," I said. "Let me talk to her tomorrow, and we'll take it from there."

❖❖❖

I waited until everyone left and Angela was still playing.

"I have friends who want to play with you. You can't see them, but you might be able to hear them. They are the Punwees, remember we talked about them?"

"You mean they're not imaginary. They're real," Angela said taking a deep breath.

"They're real. I'm sorry you can't see them. They tried yesterday to get your attention, but you didn't notice. They were disappointed. Want to see if you can hear them?" I asked.

"Okay, you won't move your lips but can you throw your voice?" she asked turning toward me. "Really, you want to go there?"

"I don't throw my voice. I'll stand right here and you can see me. Maybe you'll be able to hear them, maybe not. Do you want to try?"

"Okay, I'm game," she said. "Where do I look when I talk?"

"They'll talk to you," I said. "The first one to speak will be Dubber. Dubber, this is Angela. Angela, Dubber is standing to your right at the side of the monitor."

"Pleased to meet you," Angela said, sitting very still looking at the edge of the screen.

"It's my pleasure," Dubber said, making a bow that was lost. "Can you hear me?"

"Yes...Yes, I can," Angela said. "You voice is not very loud, but I've heard you're not very big... am I right?"

"Big enough to play games with you," Dubber said standing as straight as he could. "Angela, this is Radit. Radit, this is Angela," Dubber continued pointing toward Radit standing beside him.

"Hi, Angela, nice to meet you. Can you hear me?"

"Yes, I can," Angela said. "Their voices are different. You are not doing this." She looked at me. I sat quietly during the entire exchange.

"Angela, this is Fluw. Fluw, this is Angela," Dubber

continued.

"Nice to meet you, Fluw," Angela said. "Let me hear you talk."

"Duh...duh...duh," Fluw said, blushing a bright red and looking to Dubber for help.

"Fluw is shy," Dubber said. "Did you hear anything he stuttered?"

"I think so," Angela said. "We'll be friends, then you won't be shy. How do you play? With the controller?"

"No," Dubber said. "We use the computer keypad and the arrow keys."

"I skate on the keypad like this." Dubber skated around making the arrow move across the screen.

"I work the right arrow and the up," Radit said, making the cursor arrow jump on the screen as he moved around.

"I work the left arrow and the down," Fluw said, showing her what he could do.

"Wow, don't know what to say. But we'll play. I have to get home now. See you tomorrow," she said. She picked up her backpack, her controller, and headed for the door.

"I need to think about this," she said. "See you later."

❖❖❖

"She left all of a sudden. She okay?" Dubber asked me when I returned.

"I think so. We'll see tomorrow," I said, picking up my controller and going back to my game.

My mom suddenly appeared in the doorway with a basket of clean clothes. She crossed the room to my dresser, putting the clothes away.

"Who are you talking to?" she asked. "I heard voices."

The Punwees stopped jumping on the keys and froze.

"I was just talking to myself," I said.

"Still missing the beach?' she asked. She picked up the basket and moved toward the door. "It'll work out. Don't give up. You might need a real person to talk to. I'll speak to your dad," she said turning around and going back down the stairs before I could say anything.At supper that night, my dad said, "Mason, talking to yourself is not a good sign. We are concerned about you. You are moody and spending too much time in your room. You were more active before we moved here. We are talking about finding someone beside your mom and me to talk to. I'm going to call the school tomorrow and get the names of some counselors who would be good for you. I want you to know we're worried."

"Dad, I know I'm not as active as I was in San Diego, but there is no surfing here. I haven't found anything that I like as much as surfing, but I'll keep looking, I'm fine, just let me adjust. I was just muttering. Miss my friends. Sometimes I talk to Frisbee," I added. "He likes history so I read from my text."

"I want to know if you are having trouble. We'll get you help," my dad said. He looked concerned as he returned to his dinner.

After dinner, I explained to the Punwee trio, "We've got to be quiet. My parents want to send me to talk to someone about my hallucinations. That'd be you."

"We're not a hallucination. We're real," Dubber said. He lifted his hand up in the high five gesture that I taught him. "Up high, down low," Dubber, Radit, and Fluw jumped up and danced around.

## ELEVEN

At the bus stop the next morning before anyone arrived, Angela turned to me, "I'm not saying a word about yesterday. I'm not going to let anyone think I'm as crazy as they think you are."

"Okay," I said, greeting Ted who was walking up in his usual chaotic state.

There was nothing unusual about the afternoon. When the boys left Angela was still playing.

Angela called, "Dubber, Radit, Fluw are you going to come out and play?"

Dubber skated his response across the keypad moving the arrow in greeting. "Been waiting for you to come home."

"Good," Angela said. "I'm ready to beat you."

They played hard, but no matter the trio couldn't beat Angela. She was fast and she knew the details of game strategy. When she left, Dubber turned to me, and said, "No wonder you like to play with her. She's a master."

"Yes," I agreed, nodding. "She is the best player I've ever seen. My San Diego friends were pretty good, but not as good as Angela."

"There is something else we need to talk about," Dubber said, looking concerned and clutching his hands together. "They called a Council of Clans meeting to discuss the hunts you've been leading. Just so you know," Dubber said, turning back to the keyboard.

**December 5**

We were playing in my room. Angela involved in her competition with the trio. A sound came from under one corner of the bed, a deep cough.

"Megatherian," the deep voice began. "What is going on? Dubber, Radit, and Fluw what are you doing?" The voice was clear, distinct, and upset.

Everyone froze. The voice continued like a foghorn. "I'm Dunwartis, the Diminutive, Dust Bunny Clan leader. Dubber, Radit, Fluw, I am speaking to you. You've defied tradition. Why are you interacting with humans?"

Even Angela turned in her chair to face the direction of the voice. Dunwartis stepped further from under the bed radiating outrage. He stalked forward into the middle of the floor. Everyone was stunned and silent.

"I demand an explanation," he said, looking at Dubber then the other two.

"We wanted to play the games. We asked him to teach us," Dubber explained. "We were excited to learn about his technology."

"As son of the clan leader, you know better than to do something so forbidden," Dunwartis said. He trembled all over, raising his fist and shaking it.

"But Dad...." Dubber tried to get a word in.

"Our worlds cannot collide. When we are seen, our worlds touch. It isn't allowed."

"What's the harm?" Dubber asked.

"Mason's mother will come up here with the great wind when she finds out something is under his bed. We'll be lucky if we're not sucked up," Dunwartis raged on. He waved his arms, making fists, his face a bright red.

Dunwartis paused to collect himself. He took a deep breath. "We've lived beside humans all this time by following rules," Dunwartis said. "Dubber and his friends need to understand this. Their survival is at stake. I'll have to lead my clan out of this house and away from here. This is trouble for everyone," Dunwartis said, starting to wind up again.

"Please don't leave. Dubber, Radit, and Fluw are great. We love spending time together," I said.

"This is dangerous for us. Our history tells of complete clan exterminations," Dunwartis said. "This is the reason for our laws."

The trio chimed in. "Please, we love our games. We're learning. Some of what we learn will be of use to our culture," Dubber said. "Please reconsider, Dad."

"How will this be useful?" he said. "Explain how this will be useful to a culture without this technology." Dunwartis paused his tirade considering. "Mason is the first person to see us in recorded times. I'll have to bring this situation to the council. We'll see what they say," Dunwartis pointed under the bed. "You three better get home before I change my mind."

Angela picked up her things and went home looking pale and shaken.

❖❖❖

My mother was in the hallway when Dunwartis roared at us. "Mason," she said coming through the doorway, passing Angela. "Who is the man you are talking to?"

"There is no one in here, Mom. See, look around."

"Why was Angela in such a hurry to leave. Did you frighten her? What's going on with you?"

"Just mumbling," I said not making eye contact with her.

She stood there a minute with her hands on her hips. The Punwee trio had stopped moving, and Dunwartis froze at the bed leg.

"I'm talking to your father. You're going to see someone," she said. She turned to go, then turned back. "I've been finding your computer on during the day. Are you playing before school? Why is the computer left on? What is going on?" She left the room heading downstairs without waiting for an answer.

"Great," I said to myself. "Trouble on all fronts." I threw myself across my bed.

The Commander called and made the appointment for me that night.

"Take this opportunity to talk to this man I found. He is supposed to be very good. He will help you if you let him. Please work with him."

## TWELVE

My psychologist, Mr. Crumpini, was wrinkled, balding, and smelled like garlic. As I sat on his yellow plaid sofa, I wondered if he was warding off vampires with his strong odor.

"Chief complaint is listed as talking to yourself, possibly imagining little people. Report from parents and fourth grade teacher. Please explain why everyone thinks this," Mr. Crumpini looked up from the folder in his hands. He put the folder on the end table and picked up his pad and pen.

"Well," I started, "...my teacher thinks this because I brought a walnut to school that had a tiny door in it and told her I saw little people."

"What do little people represent to you? Your lost friends? I understand that you just moved here," he continued.

"Little people are just little people. They don't represent anything," I said, wiggling around on the sofa trying to get comfortable. "I never saw them before, how can they represent something?"

"Did you have imaginary friends when you were younger?" Mr. Crumpini droned like a buzzing bee gathering pollen. I looked out the window and wondered how long this torture would last. I drifted a little, startled when I heard my name.

"Mason...Mason, are you listening?" he said. It must have been obvious I wasn't.

"What...," I said with a start trying to orient myself.

"I had an imaginary friend when I was younger than you," he continued. "He used to help me steal cookies from the kitchen. I was an overweight boy." He looked at me for a response. But I had none. I just looked at him. This was awful.

## THIRTEEN

**April 1**

Ted and I collected insects under the giant arching rose bush at the park entrance.

"How many of the insects on the list do you have?" I called to Ted who had flopped by the rose bush. I sat down beside him.

"There are only three left on this list," Ted said, waving the paper he unfolded from his pocket.

"I'm going to rest a minute," I said reclining and smelling the flowers as the petals drifted down around me like pink snow in the warm sun.

"There's a walking stick," I pointed to a branch above my head. "Can you see it?" I watched it a minute. I saw Punwees wearing pink and green riding on the insect just like they were sitting on a bus. They had pink faces and white hair.

"Where?" Ted asked. "I don't see one."

I pointed to the green creature moving slowly along the branch above me. "Up there. Punwees are sitting on it. Can you see it? Them?"

"I don't see nothing but the walking stick," Ted said with disgust in his voice.

"Hello," I said. "What's your name?"

"Rosicough, the Stubby of the rosebush Punwees. You are Megatherian," he said.

"Can you hear them?" I asked. "They talked to me."

"No, can't hear anything. Bees buzzing," Ted said. He stared at the insect.

I turned to Ted. "You don't see the tiny beings sitting on the walking stick? They're lined up like they're riding a bus?"

"I don't see anything but leaves and rose buds, and the walking stick. Who are you talking to? I don't hear anything. How can you be so lucky?"

"It's not lucky. I'm talking to a counselor, remember. Where will you go?" I asked, turning back to the insect.

"We'll find another rose bush far from here," Rosicough said.

As we walked home, Ted kept talking about our encounter. Crossing my front yard, I saw the Commander getting out of the car.

"I can't believe you're so lucky," Ted said. I looked up and Dad was standing there.

"Hello, Commander Garcia. See you tomorrow, Mason," Ted called as he walked past.

"Yeah," I answered him, looking down hoping that Dad didn't hear the conversation.

"Come in and set the table," mom called. I hurried to the kitchen grateful for the reprieve, still not making eye contact with my father.

We sat down to dinner.

I stuffed my cheeks full of mashed potatoes and meatloaf.

"Take smaller bites, Mason, the meatloaf isn't going anywhere," Mom said, settling down to her plate.

"So," Dad began, "what were you and Ted doing in the park?"

"Nurph," I said, chewing like it was my last meal on earth. "We caught insects by the rose bush at the entrance. We had to catch five different insects for science homework."

"Well, what was Ted talking about? Your luck?"

"We played a game of tag at recess," I lied. "I've never been caught."

"Tag. Maybe you'll become a track star. I've always admired track stars. How are your sessions with Mr. Crumpini coming?"

"Okay. We talk about stuff." I finished my dinner, took my plate to the kitchen, and hurried to my room saying, "I've got homework to do."

## FOURTEEN

When Ted went back to school, he told the students that I talked to the Punwees. The boys went wild, and they wanted to see one more than ever.

"I heard him talk to them," Ted said. "He sat right beside me, talked to them. I didn't see anything, but the dumb insect he said they were riding."

"Not everyone sees them. Ted didn't see them."

"Well," Stanley said, "I want to see one. Let's hunt. Maybe I'll be able to."

Most of the boys rejoined the hunt with vigor. Oliver who had never been part of the hunts, or had anything to do with me, started the rumor that I was crazy. He caught me in the hall. "You think you're so smart, just because you're a surfer, you're better than us. How can you make up a story about tiny people, and think you'd get away with it. I'm on to you. You lying, creepy, insane, twitnit."

I stood there, listening to him, and wondered what a twitnit was.

❖❖❖

After Ted left in the afternoons, Angela played with the Punwee trio.

"You are awesome. You almost beat me that time," she said.

"I know," Dubber said. "We are getting better. We want to win."

"I'll teach you how to trash talk so you can torment Mason. Want to learn?"

"Yes, let's learn trash talk for Mason," Radit said. "How does it start?"

"You make a comment about his controller thumb, like, getting slow with that thumb, Mason. We'll beat you next time. Better keep practicing."

"Sounds like fun," Fluw said, moving his arrow key. "Trash talking is a new game."

"Yes," Angela said. "New game."

"Don't teach them that. I've enough trouble with my mother hearing voices in here without you teaching them taunts."

"How's counseling going?" Angela asked, raising her eyebrows expressing a false concern.

"Don't mention Mr. Crumpini. Ms. Rainy called my parents about the new sightings. My parents have increased my visits to weekly. I'm going to run out of things to talk about. I've covered my surfing, my current friends, and the Punwees, but he still thinks I'm struggling with a deep depression."

"They're worried about you. If I weren't in here playing with them right now, I'd worry about you too. Seeing tiny people sounds crazy," she said, diverting her attention back to the screen so she could stay ahead of the trio playing with her. "No offense guys."

"Not a hallucination," Dubber called.

"I don't know what I'm going to do," I confessed, flopping on my bed.

❖ ❖ ❖

Later that evening, I wandered down to the park. As I walked toward the pond, I saw the shadows of the soft evening light where the sand met the gently lapping water. The waterfall burbled as it dropped beneath the pedestrian bridge. I listened to tunes Ted recommended. Vines hung from the trees making the place spooky, a place of secrets and magic. I thought some of the old rock-n-roll wasn't too bad. Red 4, and the Ming Jug Band were okay, but the rest of Ted's selection required more thought, and maybe another listen. I headed up the path that led past the arching rose at the entrance.

"HEY," Dunwartis called out to me. I stopped at attention.

"Good. We were just getting ready to discuss you and my boys. Join us," he said.

"Council, this is Mason, Megatherian, Mason, Megatherian, the Council," I looked around pulling my ear buds out and shoving everything in my pocket. They were a tiny imposing swarm with serious expressions. I was startled to realize that each clan was a different color, not just clothing but bodies and hair.

"When I caught my boys, he was teaching them to play what they call video games. They seem to be having fun and weren't doing any harm, but they had violated the no contact law. They insist that learning to use the computer equipment will benefit our clans and way of life. They want us to think about adopting new ways."

"I don't know," Rosicough said. "Megatherian led the hunting parties. He can see us, and he is dangerous."

"Wait, a minute," I spoke up. "I came here from far away, a place where I rode the waves. When I arrived, I thought maybe everyone could see you, I didn't know. How was I to know I was special? I haven't been special before. I'm sorry I led the hunting parties."

Tolamar stood up and raised his hands. He had been sitting beneath the rose on a tiny bench. The murmur of voices died down to a whisper. Mosavern, a small red figure with a black beard, stepped forward.

"I am leader of the Furnace Vent clan. Ted, a boy who was with you, reported that you saw us the other day on this very bush, and the hunts have started again. What do you suggest? How can you stop this?" Mosavern strode in my direction stopping with military precision.

I stood stunned by the danger I caused.

"The matter of the Megatherian outsider is too big to be decided by the local council. We must convene the Grand Council and bring it to them. We are too close to the hunt to be objective about the megatherian," Tolamar declared. "I adjourn this meeting 'til after the next quarter moon, and we'll assemble the clans. You, Mason, will also attend. We expect you to speak and defend yourself and your customs."

I stood stunned and amazed, as they disappeared into the rose blending with the leaves and stems.

# FIFTEEN

## April 15

I waited for the Grand Council. As the Punwee clans assembled, I noticed a variety of differences in them. For one they had different ways of traveling. Their carrier birds landed by the rose bush, and waited for their passengers to disbark, and then they roosted in the trees. Some rode leaves on the wind, landing just beyond the gathering area. Some rode insects like the praying mantis, and the grasshopper.

I sat on the sidewalk, watched, and waited.

Tolamar raised his hands to calm the excited voices and their murmurs subsided. "Come to order."

Tolamar turned to address me. "Mason, Megatherian, you've seen us three different times. What have you got to say in your defense?"

"I never intended to harm you. I ask you to forgive me, because I didn't know any better," I said hoping it would be enough. "How can I make this up to you?"

Tolamar turned to the group, "Do we accept his apology? Can I see a show of hands?" Many hands raised. A silvery Punwee stood up and said, "What harm can there be to forgive him? He might even be turned into an ally if we get to know him better. I, Samvon, of the water pond Punwees, say make him our friend. See what happens."

"I'll be a good friend. I was looking for new friends when I told the boys about you," I said.

Tolamar raised his hands. "In our ancient tellings there are reports of Megatherians who are Presagers. Presagers help us survive times of persecution. Can we ask him to be our Presager?"

Samvon said, " I second the motion. Let's enlist him. He is the first person to see us in these times. There might be a reason for it."

"Aye," the crowd cried.

"Ok. We declare you our Presager. Help us avoid discovery. You'll advise us. Maybe you can think of a way to discourage the hunters or distract them, so they won't look so hard. Will you accept this duty as our protector?"

"What would my duties be?" I asked. "I want to know that I can do what you expect."

Tolamar began, "As Presager you can communicate for us. We come together every spring and hold our annual games. We want to hold our spring races in this park in peace."

"I'll try my best," I said. "I accept the position of Punwee Presager."

❖❖❖

**May 20**

The school year was winding down. We moved our afternoons to the park. I was ready for the school year to end. I wanted to put this whole crazy year behind me. I kept trying to think of a way to help the Punwees.

"Mr. Crumpini believes you are making great progress in adjusting to Blytheville." Dad began at dinner. "How do you feel about your time with him? Shall we continue the sessions, or slow them down for the summer? I'd like your opinion."

"No, I don't need any more sessions. Mr. Crumpini approves of my study habits, and my summer plans to get used to this town and my neighborhood. I'd like you to believe that I'm okay."

❖❖❖

## May 23

Two days before class day, Ms. Rainy said, "Have any of you decided how you want to spend your last day? I think we should play in the local park and have a picnic."

All of a sudden it was clear to me. I shot up my hand. "I've got an idea, which park could we go to? Can we go to the park by my house?"

"Any special reason for suggesting that park?" she said, shushing everyone.

"I'll ask the Punwees to hold their summer races that day. We can start our day by watching their games, I said, glancing around to see how my idea was received. Ms. Rainy studied me looking puzzled.

"You do remember you're the only one who can see the Punwees, don't you? Ms. Rainy said, staring with her serious face. "How can we enjoy this?"

"Everyone'll listen and create pictures in your minds. Since you can't see the Punwees, you'll have to use your imagination. You can see by listening and pretending." I looked around hoping this would work.

"Do you think you can describe them so that we can see them?" Ms. Rainy asked. "It'll be like a radio broadcast without the radio," she said. "What do you think, class?

"Yes, let Mason describe what he sees. Maybe we can see it too. We'll listen carefully," Ted volunteered. "I want to be a part of the Punwee Spring games."

"I've got to ask them. There may be things I have to do to make this happen. Let me tell you tomorrow if this will work."

Stella started to laugh, "Your going to describe your imaginary friends? You think this'll be fun? You can make us imagine them by talking? Great idea," Stella said. The other girls laughed with her.

Oliver glared at me. "Always trying to get attention."

"Since no one has a better idea," Ms. Rainy said looking around the room. "Let's see if we can work this out. Mason, we'll need to talk to your parents first."

Ms. Rainy called my parents and asked if it was a good idea to let me go ahead with my plan. My mother discussed the idea with Mr. Crumpini.

At the dinner table that night my mother introduced the subject. "Mr. Crumpini feels it will be okay for Mason to do this for the class."

My father looked at me, "If this will get you back on track, okay. Are you ready to cut ties with your imaginary world? What if the kids make fun of you? Are you ready for that?"

"Maybe I can be finished with this after class day," I said shrugging my shoulders. I didn't know if this would work. It would not work if anyone else could see them. I kept eating listening to my parents discuss my imagination. I excused myself after getting a "yes, sir, carry on." from my father.

After I finished the dishes, I walked down to the park. I stood by the rose bush and called out, "to any Punwee listening. This is your Presager speaking. I need to meet with the clan council now."

Drip, a very young Punwee, ran to tell his father, Rosicough the Stubby. "Dad, someone calling himself Presager talked out loud to the rose bush about wanting to meet the clan council. I heard him."

"Thank you, son, we'll meet him right away."

I squatted on the sidewalk and waited for the meeting. Soon among the rustle of rose leaves the clan council convened.

Tolamar began, "the Presager has the floor."

"Can the kids in my class watch your races? Since I'm the only one who can see you, I'll describe them. They'll sit around the field as spectators," I said, studying their faces to see any reaction.

"They'll listen?" Tolamar asked. "We'd have to mark off a place. I don't want to be sat on or trampled."

"You show me. I'll mark off the field. I'll ask the kids to respect you," I said. "After these games the kids will lose interest in hunting you since I'm the only one who sees you. You can live in peace."

The council voted. Tolamar turned to me, "We agree to this. We'll meet you in the park to show you boundaries."

## SIXTEEN

I took the news of the Punwee Agreement back to the Class.

"I'll mark off the field for their competition. Everyone has to respect the boundaries. I don't want any Punwees injured. We need to be good spectators."

"We'll be good, won't we?" Ms. Rainy asked the class.

"Yes!" the class shouted in agreement with only one or two grumbles.

After school I met with the council. I took my tape measure and marked off the race lanes with white tape. Red and yellow tape wrapped around stakes on the side of the race lanes formed a spectator area going up the hillside.

"If this works, then they'll think we're imaginary and give up the hunt?" Tolamar asked.

"This'll work unless someone else in my class can see you. If they can then they'll know you are not imaginary," I said. "I hope no one else can see you."

"You're the first person to see us in many cycles of history, so I don't expect anyone else to," Tolamar said.

❖❖❖

Later that evening, Angela called me. "Can you really make us see them?"

"I'm going to try. I hope this will stop the hunting. I don't care if I look like a fool. I want this to be over."

Next morning Ms. Rainy asked me. "Everything ready?"

"Yep," I nodded my head in agreement.

Arriving at the park, the children moved under my direction to their designated places by the field of competition.

"Sit between the red and yellow taped lines," I said as I pointed to the location. The students took their blankets and laid them on the grass. I took my microphone from my backpack and waited. Soon everyone was seated and waiting expectantly.

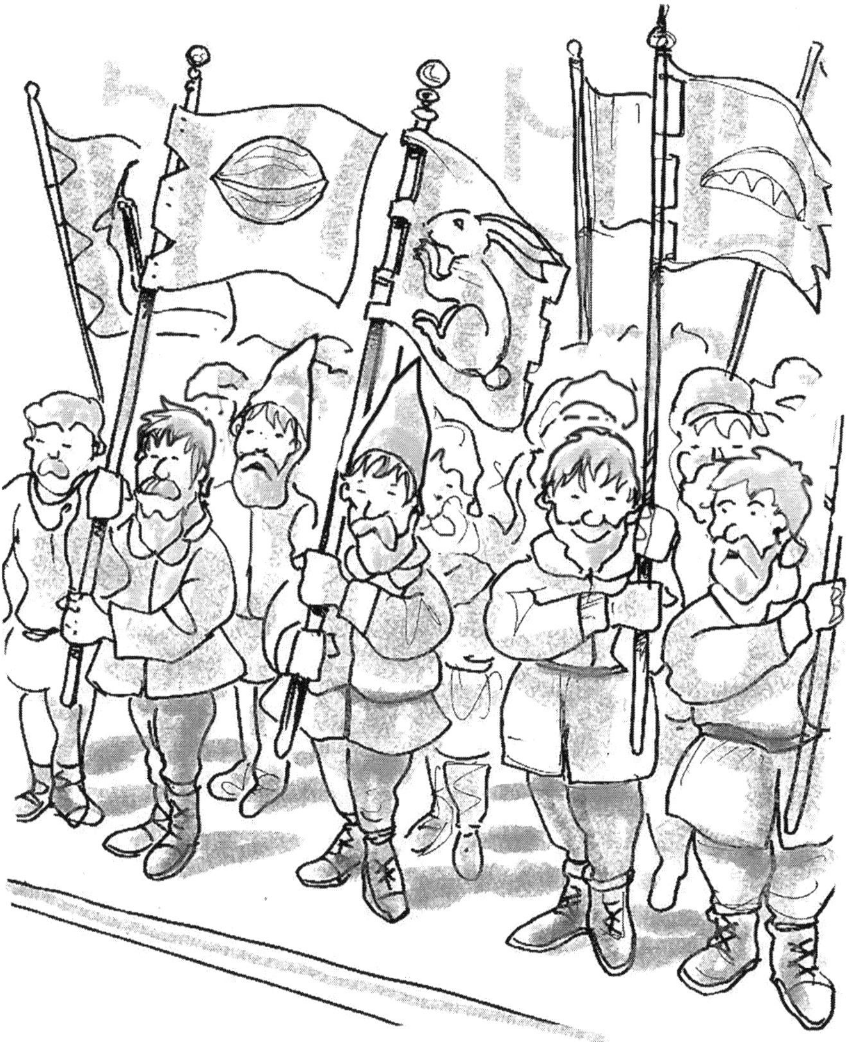

"This first contest in the Punwee Spring Races is the twenty five centimeter for individuals. The clans are marching to the starting line behind their flag bearers. I've a list of their flags. I'll describe the flag bearer of each clan so you can see their differences. The first one has a green walnut on a pale green background. The flag bearer is a brown Punwee wearing green. The next one is a tan dust bunny on a pale gray background. The bearer is yellow with yellow hair. Here comes the clan with their rock symbol on a light tan background. They are gray with black hair. Behind them is the Rose clan pink and green banner. The flag carrier is pink with red hair. Next is the red and yellow flag of the Furnace Vent clan. The bearer is red with dark brown hair. There's a brown flag with rushing waves on it for the Sewer Drain group. The bearer is brown with dark brown hair.

Just then Anna, one of the girls, jumped up and ran down the slope where everyone was sitting. She started jumping around on the racecourse yelling, "I'm going to pretend that I'm stomping them. I can't imagine them."

The Punwee parade scattered. Angela jumped up and ran down to the field shouting, "you could hurt somebody, stamping around like that!" Angela grabbed Anna by both arms.

Ms. Rainy ran down the slope to the two girls. "This is not what the class agreed to do. You'll sit quietly by yourself away from the games until they are finished. Both of you. Then we'll discuss whether we are going to let you take part in the rest of the day. I'm talking to your parents about your behavior."

Anna sniffled and followed one of the chaperones to a picnic table removed from the race area. Ms. Rainy took Angela by the arm and sat her at another.

"Mason, please start again," Ms. Rainy directed.

"Come back to the flag lineup," I called.

Tolamar walked up to me. "Are you sure this is safe?" he asked.

"It'll be safe for them to return, won't it?" I asked the class. As they shook their heads, "yes it is safe, Tolamar."

"Yes," the class called.

"Go on," Ted said.

"As the parade of flags finishes, a white flower on a blue background for the Water clan goes by. They are a blue green color with white hair. There's the black flag with the white outlet of the clan living in the tangle of cords behind entertainment systems. They are black with white hair. There's the pale blue with a cattail on it for the swamp clan. They are pale blue with brown hair. Last the white flag with the straight board for the Baseboard groups. They are white with gray hair. Can you imagine them? They are an amazing sight. I hope that you can see them in your mind."

The children listened and watched the field hoping to see one. They sat very still whispering to each other.

"In the first race, we have ten participants, one from each clan. They're wearing numbers from one to ten. The numbers are so small I can hardly see them. They've lined up at the white starting line. Can everyone see it? The runners will run down the lanes moving out from the start to the green line at the finish. See it over there?"

All the children's eyes turned toward the taped lanes. Even the girls stopped giggling to listen. I stood shifting my weight, clutching my microphone, warming up to my responsibility.

"Everyone is ready. Get set. There goes the signal. Each runner darts down the field in his lane. It's quite a distance for them. They're over half way now. They're moving fast. Coming up on the finish line. It's over! It looks like..., Oh no.. number ten falls down. I think it is, number three. Just a minute, we'll have the winner's name for you. Number five and nine are second and third." I squatted down, listening to Drip close to the ground.

"Just reported to me, the winner is Martin the Minute of the Cord clan. Good job, what a race! Second place goes to Migbit, the Rose Bush clan, and the Third place winner is Birn, the Furnace Vent clan."

"There are only two races at this time. Let's take a break before the final race of the day. We'll have a snack while the little runners get ready. Can anyone else see them?" I asked searching the crowd. I looked for a show of hands, nothing. The snack monitors passed out fruit. The kids sat in three rows of ten students. The class sat there munching their apples. I sat down and ate mine. I stood up.

"Final race is a relay. There are ten four member teams. Each member has to run twenty-five centimeters and hand off the tiny straw. If they drop the straw, they lose. All four team members have to complete their races. Oh wow, it's exciting! The first runner for each team is at the starting line. Get set. Go. They're off! It looks like team three is pulling ahead in the first leg of this race. But team six and team ten are advancing. Team three is about to release the next runner. Team six runners and team ten runners are closing fast. Just look!" I shouted, jumping up and down.

Ted yelled, "Where is clan two?"

"They are behind everyone," I called.

The entire fourth grade began to cheer. They began to chant for their favorite team. "Run fast, team two. Get with it, team ten. Let's go, team five."

Even Ms. Rainy got into the action. "Let's win, team three!"

"Team three is still in the lead. They're lightning; they're at least five centimeters ahead of anyone else. The others are closing their lead. Everyone is running hard. Their efforts are paying off. Fourth lap," I announced. "Team three leads. They're running a fast speed. Team two is trying to catch them but is half a lap behind. Team six looks like it might make third place if they keep running. What a race! Now they're coming to the finish line. Team three is ahead by at least four centimeters. They...they...they just crossed the finish line! The winning relay team is team three. Let's give a big cheer for team three, and all of the other competitors who made this race so exciting.

The fourth graders went wild.

"Hurrah for all the teams" Ted clapped. Stan jumped up and down and sang. "Team three wins. Team three wins." I raised my hands for silence and squatted down. Finally everyone quieted down and sat looking at me.

Tolamar approached me.

"Presager, tell the children we're honored to race for them. They're wonderful spectators."

I stood up and said. "Tolamar, the Miniscule congratulates the fourth grade on being wonderful spectators. The Punwee games are now over. As soon as they clear the field, we can play."

The class cheered again.

"What fun, Mason!" Ms. Rainy gave me a pat on the back. "What an imagination you have! I could see them in my mind."

❖ ❖ ❖

As Ted, Angela, and I walked home from the park, Angela turned to me.

"That was great. I could see them racing," Angela said.

"Oh, me too," Ted said.

"Thanks. Looks like a great summer for everyone," I said.

❖❖❖

I thought about the day. The class had so much fun. They played the entire day. I, the Presager, hoped the Punwees were safe. I didn't care that my fourth grade thought I made it all up.

Ms. Rainy called The Commander.

My father came into my room that night.

"Is sounds like you impressed your class today with your imagination. I don't want you to live in your imagination, but I'm glad to see you use it in a real way. I want you to make real friends. Your teacher gave you a great compliment. I'm proud of you. I'll cancel the counselor appointments."

I settled in my bed happy that I'd pleased my dad.

Dubber, Radit, and Fluw called from underneath my bed, "Good job, we'll play Aria Kingdom tomorrow. Good night."

"Good night," I whispered. I slept well knowing I'd been the best friend and Presage I could be.

## ACKNOWLEDGEMENTS

So many people have encouraged me that I'm grateful to everyone. I give you my third story. I hope you like it.

Please, please, please, review this book on Amazon and Goodreads.

**Work of mouth still makes or breaks authors.**

## BIOGRAPHY

I'm an Oklahoma girl who spent thirty years living in the deep South. I'm an observer. Everything can be the basis of a good story. Story ideas are everywhere. No need to give you my dates like I've passed from this life. I'm here. It's now. Let's read.

I write stories for children. The golden age of adventure when they can still use their imagination is between the ages of six and twelve. I love creating worlds for them to explore. Reading is so important. It is the gateway to their future.

I live with my husband and two cranky cats in northeast Oklahoma. I can be contacted:

Facebook: marytkincaidauthor

Twitter: @marykincaid2001

Pinterest: marytkincaidauthor/blogger

Website: http://marytkincaidauthor.com

Mary

Find me on Amazon: Mary T Kincaid

Like me on Facebook: marytkincaidauthor follow me on Twitter: @marykincaid2001

Follow me on Pinterest: marytkincaidauthor/blogger

First chapter of new work.

## HAWK MCCOY: THE PENTHIADS

*THE DAY SCHOOL IS OUT FOR SUMMER*
*AFTERNOON: 6/1/2013, 3:00PM TOWN-IZLET BAY*

Hawkins burst through the door of the Izlet Bay elementary school, picked up his bike, and started home. This was the last day of fourth grade, and pumping with his whole body, he sped his bike along. The afternoon sunshine lit his red hair and the exertions brought color to his cheeks as he threw gravel during his skid at the foot of his driveway. The boy stilled his bike, reached out, and pulled the mailbox door open. Empty! His summer issue of *Junior Sleuth* was not there. Frowning and disappointed, he headed to his back door. Having his new magazine would have made the day perfect. He parked his bike and lugged his backpack inside.

He reached the kitchen where his mother waited. "Hawkins McCoy, explain the black powder all over the refrigerator."

"I'm Hawk, Mom. Don't call me Hawkins. It's fingerprint dust. I practiced fingerprint collecting. I knew I could find your prints and Dad's in the kitchen. I'll clean it up." Hawk took the spray cleaner and sponge, and scrubbed. His blue eyes were shining with determination. "I'm going to learn how to collect and read fingerprints this summer. I have everything I need, to practice."

"I know you'll learn it. Wish you were doing something neater like stamp collecting." He looked up, watching his mother stand there with her hands on her hips, studying him. Her red hair was pulled up in a band. The young detective recognized her expression.

"Stamps, ugh." Hawk scrubbed the sooty residue from the white fridge, desperate to get back to his *Fingerprint Guide For All Occasions*. He put the cleaning supplies away. Next, he wanted to collect the fingerprints of his best friends, Sandy Sue South and Tom Buford.

His best friends would let him do that. The three of them had worked and played together since the first grade. They formed the neighborhood odd jobs club called The Durrett Street Indispensables Handiservice. The entire neighborhood used them for their various small jobs. Their dog-walking service was used by everyone. The money-making 'Poo Patrol' was a neighborhood legend.

"Going upstairs," he called, putting the cleaning supplies away. His mom had walked into the laundry room, where she stood folding clothes.

He threw his backpack in the back of his closet. Another year finished he was officially a fifth grader. He even felt taller, and older. He took out his microscope, set it up on his desk, and pulled out the adhesive strips with the fingerprints he had collected with the dust. He secured another envelope.

"Ok, look at the ones with dust first," he muttered to himself. He sat and studied the whorls, swirls, and loops of his mother's fingerprints. "This is a really good example." He pulled another set from the second envelope. "Ummmm, not as clear. Looks like I smudged them. Have to practice more." He sighed and stored the print examples in their separate holders. He secured his father's prints under the microscope. "Really clear with the fingerprint dust, but a real detective can slip around and collect prints without dust." Hawk pulled out his *Fingerprint Guide For All Occasions*. "Maybe there is a hint about how to get fingerprints without using dust." He looked at the index and flipped to the recommended pages. How was he going to solve a mystery this summer if he couldn't at least collect fingerprints without making a mess?

## *AFTERNOON: 6/1/2013, 4:30PM RIDGE- WHITE HOME*

Unbeknown to Hawk, the wind was blowing in his mystery. Della Rhodes was the caretaker of the house on the hill above town which was known to locals as the White Home, because of its color. The elaborate architecture from an age past spread out on the ridge, keeping watch over the community nestled around Izlet Bay. Porches wrapped all four sides of the house, reminders of a more gentile age when porch sitting was a way to pass time with your neighbors. Flowering shrubs hugged the foundation, caressing the porch visitors with their fragrance. Their riot of confetti color added to the quiet festive air of the house.

Della paced the length of the porch, facing the east where the clouds formed. Her blond hair flew as the wind picked up. She stalked to the chair, picked up the orange cat keeping her company, and sat down. The young woman wasn't just the housekeeper; she was also the Sentinel for the secret sleeping deep beneath the basement of White Home.

She consulted the printout picked up along the way to the chair. Studying it for a minute, she sighed.

"Look at the clouds," Della said. The cat purred its response. She stroked it vigorously. Annoyed the cat jumped down. Della took some deep breaths which gave her inner stillness. A big gust of wind blew over the potted fern. The crash made her jump.

"Okay, that's it. The weather is changing. There are too many storms forming in the Atlantic. There were only six for the entire hurricane season, now there are six in six weeks." She stood up straight, set her shoulders, and walked into the house without looking back at the staring cat. She crossed the floor of the kitchen, and continued down the hall to the door of the basement laboratory. She opened the door and went downstairs. To her left, at the bottom of the stairway, was a door that said: OPEN IN CASE OF EMERGENCY. She sighed hesitating. She stretched out her hand, turned the knob, and pulled the door open. The stair lights came on as she passed through the door. She descended the narrow stairway which wound down into the earth. She resolved to wake the Penthiads. She hoped this was a good thing to do. She had no one to confide in, and didn't know the consequences of her action.

When she arrived at the bottom of the stairway, she knocked on a heavy oak door that fit the arched doorway. A tiny window creaked open.

"Yes, who is it?" a voice asked.

"I'm Della, the Sentinel. I'm here to wake the Penthiads. They are needed in the outer world. My manual instructed me to come here," Della said, her voice trembling with the tears she held back.

"We are the watchers. We take care of the Penthiads while they sleep. We will awaken them. They will be with you soon," the deep feminine voice said.

Della returned from the basement to wait. She lay out clothing as her manual specified. The manual mentioned a mineral cloth, but Della didn't understand that reference.

Made in the USA
Columbia, SC
12 January 2022

Table of Contents

*MARIGOLD*

Chapter 1: Sunny . . . . . . . . . . . . . 3
Chapter 2: Nick . . . . . . . . . . . . . 8
Chapter 3: Sunny . . . . . . . . . . . . . 13
Chapter 4: Nick . . . . . . . . . . . . . 19
Chapter 5: Mike . . . . . . . . . . . . . 22
Chapter 6: Nick . . . . . . . . . . . . . 26
Chapter 7: Sunny . . . . . . . . . . . . . 30
Chapter 8: Mike . . . . . . . . . . . . . 35
Chapter 9: The Handout . . . . . . . . . . 40

## WHITE CARNATION

Chapter 10: Sunny . . . . . . . . . . . . 45
Chapter 11: Nick . . . . . . . , , , . 51
Chapter 12: Sunny . . . . . . . . . . . 58
Chapter 13: Mike . . . . . . . . . . . . 62
Chapter 14: Sunny . . . . . . . . . . . 65
Chapter 15: Mike . . . . . . . . . . . . 68
Chapter 16: Nick . . . . . . . . . . . . 73
Chapter 17: Sunny . . . . . . . . . . . 78
Chapter 18: Sunny . . . . . . . . . . . 82
Chapter 19: Mike . . . . . . . . . . . . 88
Chapter 20: Sunny . . . . . . . . . . . 92
Chapter 21: Phil . . . . . . . . . . . 103
Chapter 22: Nick . . . . . . . . . . . 107
Chapter 23: Mike . . . . . . . . . . . 115
Chapter 24: Nick . . . . . . . . . . . 120
Chapter 25: Phil . . . . . . . . . . . 128
Chapter 26: Sunny . . . . . . . . . . 131
Chapter 27: Nick . . . . . . . . . . . 138
Chapter 28: Phil . . . . . . . . . . . 144
Chapter 29: The Senior and Society Betterment
          Plan Chart . . . . . . . . . . 152

Chapter 30: Sunny . . . . . . . . . . . . 154
Chapter 31: Nick . . . . . . . . . . . . . 159
Chapter 32: Nick . . . . . . . . . . . . . 166
Chapter 33: Mike . . . . . . . . . . . . . 169
Chapter 34: Sunny . . . . . . . . . . . . 175
Chapter 35: Nick . . . . . . . . . . . . . 181
Chapter 36: Sunny . . . . . . . . . . . . 187
Chapter 37: Nick . . . . . . . . . . . . . 191
Chapter 38: Sunny . . . . . . . . . . . . 195
Chapter 39: Mike . . . . . . . . . . . . . 197
Chapter 40: Phil . . . . . . . . . . . . . 201
Chapter 41: Sunny . . . . . . . . . . . . 206
Chapter 42: Nick . . . . . . . . . . . . . 211
Chapter 43: Phil . . . . . . . . . . . . . 213
Chapter 44: Sunny . . . . . . . . . . . . 216
Chapter 45: Nick . . . . . . . . . . . . . 221
Chapter 46: Mike . . . . . . . . . . . . . 224
Chapter 47: Sunny . . . . . . . . . . . . 227

## *SUNFLOWER*

Chapter 48: Sunny: Two Years Later . . . . . . . 233
Acknowledgments . . . . . . . . . . . 237

*MARIGOLD*

Chapter 1

# Sunny

B OOM! THE SOUND was loud and deafening. Sunny's heart raced. Her body trembled, then sunk back into the faux velvet cushion. It was so realistic.

*They really do a lot with surround sound these days,* she thought.

She hadn't expected an explosion at this part of *The Second Best Exotic Marigold Hotel*, but then she had only been half-paying attention to the movie and half-daydreaming about the past few weeks.

"We did it," she mused, her mind slipping into tangential thoughts. "Finally, a movie theater devoted to the interests of Regal Crest residents. It's about time, given all the money we spend at Eastgate Plaza." Sunny didn't consider herself a political person, but she was proud of the role she played in getting this initiative going.

She looked around. Almost every seat was taken. Through the shadows, she saw people focused on the screen. She scrunched back into her seat. It was a little too low for comfort. Her aging body was bruised from when she initially sat down with a hard flop. Sunny made a mental note that they had to do better and provide senior-appropriate furnishings. She'd figure out whom to talk to about that later.

Boom! The second blast, louder and sharper, left no doubt in her mind. The characters on the screen were seated around a dinner table, laughing. Something was very wrong.

Sunny jumped up. The woman next to her had a metal walker that she had folded carefully in front of her, leaning against the back of the seats in the previous row. Now she was blocking the aisle, trying to unfold it and keep her balance at the same time.

A gray fog seemed to come from the floor and moved quickly toward the ceiling as another blast rang out. The smoke was thicker. There was a low hum of words that got louder and louder, turning into screams and pleas for help as people panicked. Some were coughing and gagging. An elderly gentleman yelled, "Fire! Fire!" A woman with an oxygen tank pulled the thin plastic tubing out of her nose and threw the metal container into the aisle.

Sunny's eyes burned as she looked to her left. The row was clogged with people leaning on canes, the more able-bodied people shoving past them. A wall of people streamed toward the back of the theater. Some were squeezed against armrests and collapsed on the floor.

There was no easy way out in that direction. Sunny quickly assessed the situation. She was in the middle of the third row. (Thank goodness she'd been postponing her cataract surgery and had to sit up close!) If she could climb over the back of the first two rows of chairs, she could exit to the side of the screen.

Sunny hadn't done anything this physical in a long time. Sure, she did some stretching exercises and yoga poses first thing in the morning, enough to get the kinks out. But lately, it was even getting difficult to get on and off the public bus, especially if the driver forgot to put the front door in a kneeling position.

"They say a little bit of adrenaline goes a long way. If I could swing my feet over the lower area where the seats are joined, I can use my arms to push up against the back rest..."

Sunny was halfway between the first and second row when the shots rang out: bang, bang, bang, bang; four even staccato beats. It was so close, her left eardrum vibrated. She quickly used the pull of gravity to force herself to the floor and flattened her body against the ground. Her cheek pressed against a kernel of popcorn. She could hear someone wheezing next to her. A high-strained voice kept repeating "Oh my God, oh my God" like a mantra. The screaming got louder in waves behind her as the footsteps and clicking sound of metal walkers quickened and intensified.

Suddenly, it was eerily quiet. Sunny had seen enough terror movies to know she should play dead. It seemed like hours had passed, but from the ticking of the wristwatch strapped on the arm that was under her face, she knew it was only seconds.

Sunny was used to being in control. Against her better judgment, she slowly lifted her head up and looked through the space between the seats. With the exception of two people plastered on the floor near her, the area at the front of the theater had emptied out. Standing just feet in front of her was a lone figure, tall and lanky. He was folded in the shadows, his black garments blending with the darkness of the theater.

Sunny froze, afraid her slight movements had caught his attention, but he was looking up, his pistol clutched in both hands and pointing toward the ceiling. Sunny had poor night vision. She had given up driving years ago. She had difficulty recognizing someone until they were close in front of her: very embarrassing when she was trying to find a seat at Bingo, and acquaintances thought they were being rebuffed. Even with the backlight of the still-running movie, all she could see was a muddied form.

She scrunched her eyes, willing them to focus. The form swayed, and as it did, a large shiny pendant slipped from underneath its shirt collar and was caught in a glitter of low light: a silver snake coiled around a pole. Where had she seen that before?

The question flitted across her mind but was quickly replaced with cold fear as she heard the click of the revolver hammer. She lowered herself down just in time as two more shots rang out toward the ceiling.

Sunny lay still. Her muscles ached, but she didn't dare move. Minutes passed. It seemed like forever before she heard hurried, firm footsteps heading toward the center of the screen and what sounded like a loud clang of a door.

Chapter 2

# Nick

Nick stuck the pistol into the thigh pocket of his cargo pants and slipped behind the screen. There were only twelve loping steps to the emergency exit that led onto Eastwick Lane, a small alley that ran behind the theater. The other stores in the shopping plaza had back doors that abutted this alley, too: the shoemaker, the jewelry store, the nail salon, Simpson Realty. But all were closed for the evening, with the exception of Breeze Coffee Pub, a Starbucks-style café that was trying to reinvent itself as a nightclub. Tonight was karaoke night. Nick was expected there in 10 minutes to spin records.

Nick took a pack of cigarettes out of his pocket before opening the door a crack, looking both ways, and slipping outside. He let a cigarette dangle from his dry lips as he leaned against the café's wall. He could just barely hear the muffled sounds of terror as it mingled with the crescendo of sirens.

He had only a few minutes to pull himself together. It wouldn't be normal for him to stay in the alley, taking a smoke, with all the activity going on upfront.

He couldn't believe what he just did. How did it get so complicated? He just wanted to put them on notice. His mind was swirling in crazy directions. He would have to tamp it down. He tapped two fingers sharply on his forehead. That always seemed to work.

He took a deep breath before tossing the half-smoked cigarette onto the ground and walking toward the front of the stores. He glanced at the side windows of the café. The light from the amber table lamps reflected on empty tables. It would be another slow night. The owner had tried everything to pick up business: poetry readings, Scrabble night, liquor license, deli menu. The simple fact was that the older people in the community would not go out much past eight o'clock at night. And he would be out of a job again — not that he was making much. It was low-level work, given that he was a college graduate. But it was enough to keep him fed and supplied with cigarettes, and to cover an occasional haircut so he would look halfway decent for interviews.

Looking halfway decent wasn't hard to do. Nick had a swarthy look: deep brown hair that swept down across his forehead; deep, dark eyes; and an Elvis Presley look that was very endearing. His long, lanky figure and warm smile contributed to the charm, although Nick noticed recently that on occasion that smile didn't come naturally and would have to be manufactured.

There was so much commotion at the front of Eastgate Plaza that no one took particular notice of Nick as he slipped into the crowd. People were spilling from the theater into the parking lot, stunned but relieved looks on their faces. What had happened? They were relaxed and comfortably watching the movie, and the next thing they knew...

A small trickle of people was still exiting the door as a number of policemen pushed passed them and entered the interior. Two ambulances pulled up to the curb, their sirens blaring and lights flashing. One EMT hopped from the vehicle and started setting up a makeshift triage center. The others fanned out into the crowd, their medical bags in hand, to get a handle on what kind of assistance was needed. There were people scratched, bruised and coughing. A few were stunned, their hearts racing and breathing heavily.

At first glance, it looked like there were no fatalities, or serious injuries, for that matter. Suddenly, a loud piercing voice came from the center of the crowd: "Help! Please help! My husband. Please! Over here." An EMT rushed toward the direction of the cries. An elderly woman was kneeling over a prone body, her silk turquoise shirtwaist dress splattered with blood. "He can't walk well. He fell and was pushed under. It was frightening, the shoving and not being able to get up or move. It scared him. It scared me. I think it's his heart."

The crowd swelled as people in the vicinity left their homes and came to gawk. It's amazing how quickly news travels in a small community.

It was less than two years ago when a father-and-son sniper team had terrified the area just for the heck of it, taking down a shopper at Eastgate Plaza one day, shooting another at Appleway Mall the next, and targeting a teenager at the gas station a week later. The community was terrorized for months until the perpetrators were caught. People stopped shopping at the plazas and were quick to fill their tanks and leave, looking warily about as they pumped.

Nick walked along the outskirts of the crowd, listening to snippets of conversations, being sure to keep his footsteps measured. No one glanced his way. No one seemed to suspect that he had created this mayhem.

*I did this. I'm responsible for all of this*, he thought, then looked about him. He could feel a half-smile twitching on his lips. At the same time, the enormity of all of it tumbled through his brain.

*I have to think. I have to think.*

The thoughts rumbled through his mind so loudly, he was sure they could be heard. He looked over his shoulder and around the crowd. No one was paying attention. But then he saw the stretcher. A man, pale and wan, his gray hair in wisps around his face, wearing beige khakis and a matching polo shirt, was being lifted into the ambulance. Next to him was Abigail Martin, her stockings rolled up at the knees and showing under her blue dress as she tried to negotiate climbing the lift into the ambulance and hold her pocketbook at the same time. Even from that distance, Nick could see the distress on her face.

Nick caught his breath. "Mrs. Martin?" he whispered to himself. "I didn't mean to hurt anyone." He had to stop himself from physically crumbling into his body. "I just wanted to give them a good scare, so they would do something."

A sudden pain gripped the top of his head like a vise, causing Nick to visibly tremor. "Stop. Until later. Until later." Nick inhaled deeply and tapped his forehead with two fingers.

# Chapter 3

# Sunny

Sunny was pretty confident that the shooter had left, but she didn't dare move. It would be difficult to get up in either case: her body was aching, twisted like a pretzel, and tightly sandwiched in.

What had happened? It didn't make any sense. She assumed there had been some kind of smoke bomb. And then she saw the man with the gun. But why was he shooting at the ceiling instead of into the crowd?

*Lucky for me. Lucky for all of us.*

Sunny loved to problem-solve. But these were questions she would rather not have been faced with.

There were heavy footfalls at the back of the auditorium, and then along the side aisles. A deep voice yelled, "All clear," and the center lights were turned on, flooding the theater.

"Are you all right, Miss?" The policemen had fanned out and were checking all the rows.

"Yes. Yes." Despite the situation, Sunny was a little embarrassed to be found this way: unkempt and disheveled. She wasn't a vain person, but she tried to keep herself current, and felt guiltily happy that she was aging gracefully. She was thin and still had a smooth complexion that she highlighted with light makeup. Her hair was platinum-white, cut short and framing her face. Surprisingly, she even got street compliments now and then, although not like when she was younger. These days, they were more like "Mama. Looking good." Once, she was propositioned at a Walmart parking lot: "I have a truck over there: We can go and do IT." But, despite the crow's feet that were beginning to appear at the corners, it was her sparkling eyes and effervescent personality that had garnered her the nickname, Sunny, that radiated youth.

Sunny unconsciously lifted her hand and smoothed her hair before reaching her arms out to be pulled up. The policeman held her tight until she regained her balance, then wrapped his arm around her back to steady her as he walked her out of the building.

Sunny was overwhelmed with what she saw in front of her. The people milling around were the same ones who had been standing in this same spot gleefully anticipating a relaxing evening out just moments before. She should be used to it now (it happens often with older people), but she still found it amazing how things can change so much in a split second. There was Lucy Brown and Madge Simpson. Madge's husband must have come to pick her up. He looked like he'd thrown a pair of shoes on under his pajamas. And there was Anna from her yoga class; and Steffi, who she usually saw on the casino bus. Sunny's eyes swept across the crowd. And there was that nice fella, Nick, the grandson of Mae Jackson.

She remembered the first time she met Nick. Her heart had stopped in her chest, and not because it was so rare to see a handsome young man in her neighborhood—with his good looks, and if she had been younger, he would definitely have been a heartthrob—but because he reminded her so much of her son: they had the same build, the same carriage. But it was the way he related to his grandmother that touched her soul, causing the memories to come flooding back.

She had never been close to Mae; she tried to keep at arm's length the people who were tenants in her four rental properties. But she found herself finding excuses to drop by. It wasn't hard. She was Mae's landlord, after all. Of course, she would be concerned and want to make sure that everything was as it should be, especially given what happened shortly after Mae's illness.

Through her visits, she got to know Nick; his warmth and caring was so much like her son Marvin's. And as her visits got more frequent (a casserole here, a repair needed there), she felt closer to Nick. And Nick was getting to know her. She had stepped into their lives. She was sure he appreciated her support. And he seemed to be treating her in a special way, too.

She knew deep down that this wasn't healthy, trying to fill the deep void that had become a permanent part of her being by trying to foster a relationship with Nick to make up for the loss of Marvin. The whole thing was wishful thinking on her part. And it was crazy to be jealous of Mae, given her medical condition, but she just couldn't help herself. She would put herself in Mae's shoes in a minute if it meant having Marvin back.

Sunny waved her arm in Nick's direction. "Nick. Nick." The policeman loosened his grip, relieved there was someone who could take over for him.

"Nick!" Sunny called louder. She was close enough for him to hear. He seemed to be lost in a fog. She was surprised to see him there. Perhaps *The Second Best Exotic Marigold Hotel* appealed to some younger people, after all.

Just as she was about to give up, Nick turned around and seemed to recognize her. Sunny waved more frantically. She understood she wouldn't be able to extricate herself from the policeman unless he thought he was leaving her in capable hands. A rush of relief went over her as Nick began walking in her direction.

"Oh, Nick," Sunny leaned in towards Nick. His shirt was damp with sweat, and there was a burnt smell about him.

Nick took Sunny's elbow. The policeman tilted his head and walked off. Nick followed him with his eyes before turning back to Sunny.

"Mrs. Meyers. I'm glad you're okay. I was on my way to work." Nick addressed Sunny in a level way, but his eyes darted about him.

"Please call me Sunny." The protest automatically slipped from Sunny's lips. Of course, Nick would be deferential to an elder. She had raised Marvin to be that way, too. She should appreciate these polite gestures from the younger generation (like when someone gets up on the bus to give her a seat), but even though she would be 68 in a few months, it made her feel so old.

It was silly to focus on what Nick called her, given the circumstances. She quickly added, "You weren't in the theater?"

"No, I'm deejaying tonight over at the Breeze Café. I have to be there in a few minutes."

Sunny looked around her and sighed. The crowd was thinning out. "I can't believe what just happened. We had worked so hard to finally get the management to agree to a screening of a film that would appeal to my generation, and now this. I guess your grandmother wouldn't have been here…?"

"No, well, you know…"

"Yes, a shame. But maybe for the best, given this."

They stood side by side, both looking about them and lost in their own thoughts. Her husband, Joe, could never understand how someone as outgoing as Sunny could feel so comfortable with these pregnant moments. Whenever there was a pause in conversation, he felt he had to jump in and say something.

"Why don't you keep up your end of the conversation?" he protested.

"I'm comfortable listening. I'm comfortable with silent spaces. It's who I am."

Nick suddenly snapped out of his reverie. "I should be heading on." He reached into his pocket for his cell phone to check the time, and felt the cold metal of the gun instead. He pulled his hand out with a start.

"Will you be okay?"

"Yes. Yes." Sunny could hear herself sounding doubtful, so she reached over to give Nick a hug. Her head reached his shoulders. As she pulled back, she noticed a silver chain glittering around his neck.

Sunny kept her eyes on Nick's back as he walked to the cafe. He definitely had the same loping walk as her son. But something else about him was in the back of her mind. What was it? She hated getting old. It seemed that more and more, she was having trouble recalling words or the names of people, or even making connections in her mind. Why, just yesterday, she was talking to her friend Maria about their local congressman, and she couldn't for the life of her remember his name.

Sunny's thoughts got sidetracked. What was it again?

Chapter 4

# Nick

Nick walked at a measured pace towards the café. He'd have to be more careful. There weren't many people who knew him in the community; but running into Mrs. Meyers, of all people, could have been an issue. On the other hand, perhaps it was for the best to be identified and pinpointed as an innocent bystander.

Innocent bystander. He liked the ring of those two words.

Nick pushed through the café's screen door. Vince was leaning on the counter by the register in the empty room, his chin cupped in his hand.

"See the commotion? Unbelievable! Guess there's no need to set up today."

"What happened?" Nick pulled a wooden chair out and sat on it backwards, trying to control the emotions on his face.

"I don't know exactly. People said there was a smoke bomb, and then some shooting. No one seems to be hurt, though. It's just scary stuff. People are saying that it's like a copycat of that Aurora kid. You know in Colorado, the *Batman* movie. Wait, maybe there's something on the news."

Vince picked up the remote and held it toward the large flat screen TV that was on the wall. "No, nothing yet." He clicked through a few channels before turning the TV off. He stirred uncomfortably and took a few deep breaths.

"You know, now is as good a time as ever. I was just going through the books. I just can't afford to keep you on any longer. There's not enough business, even on a normal night."

Vince pushed an envelope in Nick's direction. "I'll pay you for tonight, but really, there is no need for you to stay. I can handle the crowd if anyone comes."

Nick took the envelope and rolled it between his two fingers. At $8 an hour, there would be $24 in the envelope. Added to what was in his wallet, he would only have $75 until he could find some more work.

Nick wasn't surprised. He saw this coming. Nevertheless, a wave of anger rushed over him. He dug his hand into his pocket and wrapped his fingers around the gun. He knew the stories of people going on shooting rampages at their work sites when they had been let go from their job. He understood that.

How easy it would be for him to be one of those guys. But that wasn't him. It wasn't Vince's fault that he had no business and Nick was out of work. But Nick knew whose fault it was and how to fix it.

Nick unwrapped himself from the bar stool, waved the envelope in Vince's direction, and headed towards the door. He didn't quite know how to say goodbye, but there was no need. Vince was pretending to be busy focusing on reorganizing the bar glasses on the mirrored shelves.

*He'll never know what a close call he had*, Nick thought. That idea made him feel powerful and in control. It took away the sting.

Nick exited the cafe, walked toward the back alley, and pulled out his phone. He turned it on and pushed the number 3 on his speed dial.

"I'm ready," he said in a determined voice, then quickly hung up.

# Chapter 5

# Mike

MIKE CLICKED OFF his cell phone and stood silent for a moment, as if in prayer, feeling the weight of the instrument in his hands. A slow smile spread across his face. "Yes! Yes! Yes!" His mind vaulted.

Hearing Nick's idea felt like a turning point in his life. Finally, there was something he could sink his teeth into, a project that would make a difference.

He had been ready to go ahead and implement the plans without Nick if he had to, but having him on board was much better and very satisfying. After all, Nick was the brains behind the operation. Sure, Mike was good at carrying things out, following things through, and making things happen. But Nick's ability to analyze and think outside the box was priceless.

Nick also had the uncanny ability to blend into any situation. He wasn't like Mike, who couldn't help looking like a "bad boy". His physical presence alone took all the air out the room, and Mike liked it that way. He was over six feet tall, stocky, broad and muscled. It didn't help that his arms and chest were covered with colored tattoos.

Mike had once been a tall, skinny bean pole, with thick Coke-bottle glasses—the laughing stock of the senior class of Franklin High School, and the butt of social media jokes. He tried to ignore it and take it in stride. That is, until he noticed a group of girls peering into their smart phones, twittering and pointing at him. He rushed the crowd, snatching a phone from the girl closest to him. There on the six-inch screen was himself in all his glory. The pictures had been taken surreptitiously on his last visit to the john. Mike turned beet-red, dashed the phone to the ground, and ran out the schoolyard.

The shame quickly turned to anger. Mike wasn't one to feel sorry for himself. He wasn't going to be one of those statistics who became despondent and considered suicide when being technologically stalked. Instead, he believed in the adage, "Fool me once, shame on you. Fool me twice, shame on me." He began the process of remaking himself.

Instead of continuing at Franklin, he dropped out and enrolled in an evening GED class. He spent his days lifting weights at the gym until his biceps popped from his skin. He topped off his new physique at the tattoo parlor with sayings and pictures that were borderline depraved and lewd. He shaved the hair off his head and kept it smooth and oiled. Finally, he traded in his glasses for steel-blue contact lenses that made his eyes sharp, pointed and disarming.

Mike walked over to the closet door and glanced at himself in the mirror. He liked what he saw. It was a look that was very effective and served him well. It would work for this current project too, especially when it came to recruiting new people to the fold.

Mike put his cell phone on the dresser, sat down on the narrow twin bed, and looked about him. This was his room, one of four rooms in the shared home. Its size was approximately 10 by 12, feet, not the smallest but not the biggest, either. There was a low futon against the opposite wall and a small flat screen TV that Mike bought with his first unemployment check. In the center of the room was an orange shag rug left by a former roommate. A worn card table, folding chair and metal file cabinet completed the décor.

*$400 a month for this dumpy room,* Mike thought, *along with kitchen and living room privileges. And I can barely afford it. But that will change.*

Finding work hadn't been easy. Finally, he lucked out with an entry-level position at Home Depot. It was hot the day of the interview, and he was wearing a tight short-sleeved t-shirt that emphasized his build. He was given the once-over and assigned to the gardening department for the heavy lifting of plants and terracotta pots. Mike didn't mind. Besides the money, he welcomed the opportunity to keep building his strength. But a few months later, he was out of work again. It seems that with the recession, gardening was a luxury many homeowners could no longer afford.

For a while, he hung out with the Mexicans waiting for day work. They would swarm the station wagons that drove up while he would sit on an overturned oil drum, reading a book. (He was an avid reader, a trait left over from his nerdy days.) Inevitably, the group would be sidestepped, and he would be picked for work, only, he figured, because he was white. He hated the feeling of seething resentment as he was driven away. He began going to the pickup spot only on days he was really desperate for cash.

Mike took a hefty key ring out of his pocket, got up, and walked over to the pewter file cabinet. Using the smallest key, he opened the lock and flipped to a folder in the top drawer, carefully pulling it out and spreading it open on the cardboard table. This was the blueprint. This was the plan that would change lives.

# Chapter 6

# Nick

Nick opened the apartment door carefully and slipped inside. It was only 10 PM, but he knew the whole building was probably asleep. Certainly, his grandmother was. She was sprawled out on the couch fully dressed, a woolen crochet blanket tossed across her chest. Nick sat on the deep burgundy and gold-trimmed hassock by the door, and pulled off his shoes out of habit—in homage to his grandmother. Most of the people in the complex had carpeting, but his grandmother took pride in the wooden floors she had installed and used to insist that no one walk on them with street shoes.

As Nick picked up his shoes, one slipped out of his hand and dropped on the floor, making a hollow sound.

Mae opened her eyes. "Nick, is that you?"

"Yes, grandma."

"What are you doing here?"

"I live here."

"You do?" She knitted her brows.

"How is school going?"

"Grandma, I graduated a year ago. I'm staying here with you while I look for work."

"You must be hungry. Let me make a sandwich to take home with you." Mae sat up and swung her feet to the floor.

"That's okay, grandma." Nick sat down next to Mae and put his arm around her shoulder, giving her a gentle hug. "Did you take your medicine?"

"What medicine?" Mae wiggled her way from under Nick's shoulder in protest. "I don't take medicine!"

Nick reached over to the plastic pillbox he had left on the coffee table. The pink and orange pills were still under the Thursday tab. "I'll get you some water."

Nick went into the kitchen. The sink was filled with empty Tupperware containers. The dinners he had left in the refrigerator for Thursday, Friday and Saturday were gone. Shit! He'd have to make them all over again.

Mae was standing behind him, surveying the room around her, a quizzical look on her face. "Did I eat yet? I better get something to eat."

"It's okay, grandma. The dinner food is gone. See, you're supposed to put an 'X' right here when you have something to eat. That will help you remember." Exasperated, Nick took the red marker and crossed out Thursday on the chart that was posted on the refrigerator.

He looked around him and sighed. All the walls were covered with notes: some, he had written; some were in Mae's handwriting.

Things to Do Today. Check When Done:
Brush Teeth.
Get Dressed.
Eat Breakfast.
Watch *Live with Kelly*.
Nick is here. Be back tonight.
Book is on desk.
TURN OFF STOVE.
Did you turn off the stove? Check again!
I love you. See you later. Nick.

The notes probably helped, but Nick noticed there were more of them posted than just days ago. It was clear that Mae was trying hard, but she was having more and more trouble keeping up.

Mae had known something was wrong. The night before, she had looked up her symptoms on the internet: pain in the shoulders, nausea, heart flutters. But it seemed it could wait. The early-morning heart attack had wiped out her short-term memory. She couldn't remember from moment to moment what had happened minutes before.

Nick's mind went to a dark place. *I guess that's my fault, too. Most people grandma's age wouldn't have been using a computer. I taught her. I thought it would be important for her to know how.*

Nick poured a glass of water and gave Mae her pills, watching her intently to be sure she swallowed them. He had come to live with Mae shortly after the heart attack, but he didn't know how long they could keep going this way. Mae really needed full-time care. Many of her neighbors had caretakers, but Mae couldn't afford it. Nevertheless, it was working out for him, and he was glad he could stay here. He couldn't afford an apartment on his own, especially now. The only problem was how long he could stay as a resident in a 55+ community. Usually, the limit was three months. So far, the landlady, that lady, Sunny, was looking the other way.

"It's late, grandma. Let me get you ready for bed."

"Now, you know you're my favorite, Nick. And I like having you around. But I know you have studying to do and the work-study internship. How is that cute girl you showed me a picture of?"

Nick's mind flashed to Cheryl smiling into the cell phone camera, her eyes wide and focused, her hair tousled in the wind.

"I can think of better things you can do than hang out with your grandma."

"OK, grandma. You're right. I'll go. Just as soon as I tuck you in." Nick decided to humor Mae. She won't remember any of this anyway when she sees him at the breakfast table in the morning.

# Chapter 7

# Sunny

Sunny kicked her shoes off at the foyer and hung her keys on a hook by the front door. She padded across the apartment, her feet sinking into the deep carpeting, past the dining area and through the living room. She then stepped out onto the balcony, lowering herself into a cushioned wicker chair. The heat from the daytime was still thick in the air, but she could feel it getting breezier and crisper. Her body relaxed, and she could feel her muscles unwind. What a day!

She looked blankly ahead of her, deep in thought. Across from her window was a forested area, thick with evergreen trees and low-lying foliage that camouflaged Cutter Avenue, just yards away. Ambulances and police sirens were required to turn off their flashing lights and alarms when they entered Regal Crest property (although the discreet notes posted in the lobby with death and funeral notices were reminders of the inevitable, as stark as a siren would be). She loved that even though she was so near to a major road, she could hear the hum and chirps of crickets and birds. Even the wildlife seemed to be confused between what was city and country. There was a family of deer that seemed to have taken up residence by the outside fence. Sunny had seen a red fox scurry beneath the bushes just the other day.

It was at times like these when Sunny missed Joe the most. This was his favorite place: sunk into the black leather recliner with his legs splayed, a cold beer by his side.

It was hard for Joe too when Marvin died. It was so unexpected and sudden. Joe just fell apart. He confided in Sunny that he felt guilty, and blamed himself for the accident. He had gone with Marvin to the lot to pick out a car. Marvin was prepared to settle on a sensible, sturdy, and moderately priced car; but he kept wandering over to the sporty convertibles, stopping to stroke the polished surfaces longingly. Joe called him out on it. Why not buy the car he wanted? He had a good job and could afford it. "You only live once," he said then.

"If only I hadn't talked him into buying that car," Joe said to Sunny as they lay side by side on the bed, their bodies stopping short of touching. "He was so heady with that car. He felt invincible. He took risks." Sunny reached her hand over to link Joe's fingers in hers, but he recoiled and turned on his side.

After, when she was going through Joe's personal effects, Sunny found out that Joe had done more than talk. He had lent Marvin $5,000 toward the car's purchase price. From the way the promissory note was written, Sunny knew he really meant it to be a gift—there was no due date, and the interest rate was at zero.

Sunny sighed as she thought about Joe's relationship with Marvin. It had been very trying when Marvin was little. Sunny remembered the time when Marvin, a block before reaching the nursery school, stubbornly refused to go further, and Joe physically dragged him across the threshold; and all the times Joe's anger got the best of him if Marvin was disobedient. To Sunny, Marvin was just being a child. Joe felt guilty and contrite then, too, but the difference was that, early on in their marriage, he would let Sunny console him.

Joe and Marvin were both a little hot-tempered. But as adults, they had a better relationship. Marvin would come to Joe for advice. They shared the same interest in the History Channel. Marvin patiently showed Joe how to use a smart phone; and they texted, traded photos, and shared tidbits of information on a daily basis.

Sunny could have been jealous of this sudden closeness, but she was glad that Marvin was getting to know the better side of Joe, the man she loved. She was happy for Joe, too. Besides, she and Marvin always had a special relationship. They say that sons are especially connected to their mothers, and if that's true, it really applied to her. Marvin was always sweet and attentive, not completely self-absorbed like many kids when he was growing up. They spoke on the phone every day. He genuinely cared about her, asking how her day was going, and listening to petty gripes she might share. Sunny would stop herself for a minute in the middle of a conversation with Marvin to remind herself that she was talking to her child and not another adult. She remembers talking to her own mother when she was Marvin's age, and it was all about Sunny. It never occurred to her that her mother would have thoughts and concerns she might have wanted to share.

Joe continued to struggle with his angst, and Sunny couldn't seem to help him. She could feel him slipping further and further away. On the outside, they were still the enviable couple. People at Regal Crest used to tease them because it seemed they were always together. If Sunny went walking without Joe, someone would ask, "Where's your better half? Where is Joe? What is he doing?"

Sometimes, Sunny could just close her eyes, wrap her arms around herself, and think about being in the warmth of Joe's arms. But that was long ago, long before Joe's death. Joe gave up on intimacy after Marvin died. It was almost like he didn't have a right to have those feelings anymore.

Sunny knew that many of the widowed ladies at Regal Crest wished they were in her shoes. Having a man for company and support was a sought-after commodity. Sunny overheard the men who lunch together in the Patio

Room talking about how they were being chased by women. One said he was handed a note with a phone number and the words "Call me when she's gone," when his sickly wife turned her head.

But the reality was there was no intimacy for Sunny the last five years of Joe's life. Sunny thought it was probably harder being lonely in a marriage, having a warm body next to you that you can't reach out to. It was easier now being truly alone. Sunny's place in the world was clear.

Sunny shook herself out of her reverie. *This isn't helpful.* Sunny shuffled toward the kitchen. She closed the flaps on the Venetian blinds. She checked the burners and oven, and made sure the faucet was turned off. She turned out the lights behind her as she headed toward the bedroom. She changed into her pajamas and climbed into bed, pulling the cover over her head. The day's events streamed across Sunny's mind like a fast-paced movie. She let her mind loose to follow its own chain of thoughts as she slipped into sleep.

Hours later Sunny woke with a start. She could barely breathe. Her skin felt tight and clammy. The glittering snake on the silver rod had been front and center in her dreams.

"That was Nick! That was Nick with a gun in the theater!"

# Chapter 8

# Mike

Mike took the file folder and spread the contents over the small card table. They were a small group of people on board so far, but look what happened in Egypt: a small kernel of an idea changed a nation. He was confident that once the word got out through social media, their plan would quickly take hold.

Mike thought about the incident that was in the news only this morning. A teenager in Idaho, when inviting friends to her birthday party through Facebook, had accidentally made the invitation public. 1,000 people showed up. They had to call the police to break up the crowds. And that was for something relatively unimportant — imagine what would happen when they reached out with a problem and solution that was so important to young people's lives.

He was so glad he had met Nick. Nick had been behind him on the unemployment line. They got to talking, and Mike enjoyed the conversation so much, he hung around for Nick to finish and invited him for coffee. They had covered just about every topic in the 45-minute wait, and had settled on the unique difficulties of young people of their generation by the time they got to the front of the line.

At Starbucks, the conversation got more heated without the restraints of so many people within earshot.

Nick methodically put his sugar and cream in his cup, carefully removed the paper from the stirrer, and watched the foam dissipate as he slowly stirred the tan liquid, deep in thought. He looked over Mike's way, a half-smile on his lips and with penetrating eyes. Mike caught his breath and could feel a slight shift in the atmosphere as Nick pulled his chair closer and leaned toward him on one elbow.

"You know, I've been thinking about it, and I've found a solution."

Mike leaned in close to Nick as he was lowering his voice. It was difficult to hear him with the chatter about them.

"It's very simple. There's just not enough resources for everyone... not enough to go around for the young and the old."

Mike nodded just enough to encourage Nick to go on.

"It should be our time, but instead, all the benefits are being given to the older generation: Social Security, Medicare, pensions. They drain the wealth and die, anyway.

"And what about the Walmart greeters, department store cashiers, not to mention the doctors and lawyers and other professionals who have no intention of retiring? They are taking good jobs that could be available to you or me.

"And now, with all these baby boomers getting old, it's only going to be worse."

Nick paused to catch his breath before going on.

"Our politicians are stupid, on both sides of the aisle. They think that just by tweaking the system, they can make a difference. Well, that's bullshit, and they know it.

"In this life, we have 70 good years if we're lucky, and that's it. We spend so much money trying to extend it another 10, 20, 30 years, and for what?

"The politicians are wrong. The older people are not moochers—they worked hard their whole lives for their benefits, but it is the societal structure of paying these benefits that drain resources and doesn't allow for support of the young.

"You and I are getting it at both ends—not enough to live a functional life at the beginning or at the end."

Nick looked around him and lowered his voice even lower. "You know Regal Crest?"

"Yes?" Mike's response was almost a question.

"7,000 people, just waiting to die. Do the math! Each senior annually receives an average of $15,000 in Social Security payments, plus $20,000 pension, plus $3,000 spent on Medicare, for a total of $38,000. Multiply this by the 20 years they would be receiving these payments, from ages 70 – 90, and the total is $760,000 per person. Add to that the average $50,00 left to heirs, and that totals $810,000 per person that could be better spent by us. That's almost 1 million dollars a person!"

Nick looked around the room again.

"Now take Regal Crest with its 7,000 people: 7,000 x $810,000 = $5,670,000,000 that could be diverted to the millennial generation from this community alone. And this is a conservative estimate. Many seniors live well into their 90s, and have much larger pensions and assets approaching a quarter-million if you include the value of their homes."

"So, you're saying…" Mike felt a tiny twitch in his stomach, anticipating where this was going.

"My 83-year-old grandmother lives there," Nick continued. "And do you know what her day is like? Just surviving, just eating enough food and getting enough sleep to get by another miserable day. Seventy good years should be enough. Everyone could agree. That's the dramatic change we need. We could do it here. Regal Crest could be the prototype for the rest of the country."

Nick leaned back in his chair and scanned Mike's face. A slow smile spread across his own face, followed by high-pitched laughter. "Just kidding, of course."

The conversation switched to other subjects, but Mike couldn't concentrate. His mind kept going back to Nick's proposal. What exactly was Nick saying? If it was what he was thinking, it was a bold stroke, out there, scary and definitely very wrong. It was an understatement to say it would be a big change. But the payoff could be huge. He waited for Nick to turn to that topic again, but he never did.

Back home, later that day, when he turned on his computer, an email was waiting for him from Nick, with the subject line "This IS The Plan". Attached was a document laying out what Nick had talked about in great detail. Mike immediately printed it out, deleted it from his computer, and emptied out his virtual trash can.

Now Mike shuffled through the papers to locate the packet of 15 or so pages stapled together. He'd get a group of people together for a meeting in the morning. But first, he'd have to summarize this document to talking points that people could understand.

Two hours later, he had a handout he was satisfied with. The tone was just right: presenting the problem with just a hint of the gruesome solution. You can never be too careful.

# Chapter 9

# The Handout

### MILLENNIALS VS BABY BOOMERS

### The Problem

There are not enough resources for both old people and young people.

Young people are:

- Unemployed
- Have access to fewer jobs with future prospects
- Unable to find a decent, reasonably priced place to live
- Unable to accumulate enough savings to live comfortably

Old people are:
- Draining resources, especially in the last 20 years before they die, yet these resources don't necessarily mean a better quality of life
- Increasing the deficit with healthcare costs and Medicare
- Depleting Medicaid to cover long-term care costs
- Staying at jobs longer
- Taking jobs that could be given to young people
- Draining the assets in the Social Security program
- Sitting on their own assets that could be passed down to millennials

Did You Know?
- Every day, 10,000 baby boomers turn 65
- The population aged 65 and over is projected to nearly double over the next three decades.

Do the Math
- Each senior gets an average of $38,000 annual income (15,000 social security, 20,000 pension, 3,000 Medicare) x 20-year life span (ages 70 – 90) = $760,000

- Each senior averages $50,000 in assets that could be left to heirs
- This totals $810,000 per person or $810 million for every 1,000 seniors, or $5,670,000,000 for the 7,000 seniors who live in Regal Crest, for example.

The Solution

- The solution is right under our noses
- As millennials, let's make a commitment to nip the problem in the bud
- Let's use our county as a prototype of what can be done across the country.

*WHITE CARNATION*

Chapter 10

# Sunny

SUNNY SAT UP in bed. Her heart was beating heavily in her chest. She looked around the darkened room. A sliver of light from the street lamp below her window came through the Venetian blinds. Tiny blue, red and green lights glimmered from her smoke detector, cable box, and clock radio. It was 4:44 AM.

Lately, she'd been having the strangest dreams. They'd always been detailed and colorful, but as she got older, they'd gotten worse. She even found herself once with her legs dangling over the bed. And she had screamed out loud a couple of times. "Piercing screams," Carla, whose apartment shared her bedroom wall, had said.

The dreams seemed so real, but their memory evaporated quickly. Now, as usual, she was having trouble remembering. But the feeling of fright still remained. Her skin was so sweaty that her pajamas were damp. Sunny strained to keep the thread of thoughts in her mind. "What was it that woke me?" She lay back down on her bed, her eyes on the ceiling, her legs and arms spread out like a beached whale. She began to methodically go through snippets of thoughts, beginning with yesterday's events.

"The day had started out so well. I had been so looking forward to the screening of *The Second Best Exotic Marigold Hotel* and the culmination of all the work I put in. What a great idea it was, and what a good turnout.

"But then the most horrible thing happened: the explosion, the shooting. We were lucky to get out alive.

And I was so close to the shooter, close enough to see that he was wearing a silver necklace on his neck."

Sunny jerked her body to a sitting position on the bed, breathing hard, her eyes darting around the room. "That was Nick. That was the necklace I've seen Nick wear."

She frowned. "But I saw Nick right after. He was by the Plaza. Maybe I'm remembering the necklace because he was wearing it then."

Sunny closed her eyes tight to try and recreate the scenario in her mind. All she could see was Nick being so kind and comforting, taking her arm. And then she saw Nick fade into Marvin, and fade back to Nick again. "It couldn't have been him," she thought defiantly. "Or could it?"

She sighed and looked over at the clock again. It's now a little after five. She should get up and begin her day. Perhaps a cup of coffee would clear her mind.

An hour later, nothing had changed, except she now had a low-grade headache. Sunny went into the bathroom and rummaged through the medicine cabinet, looking for an aspirin or Tylenol. She smiled when she saw the red-and-yellow color scheme she had used to accessorize, colors similar to those medicines' bottles. It had been fun decorating her new apartment when she moved here. Sure, many residents had trouble coming to Regal Crest, knowing this might be their last move and that the only reason there was a vacancy in the community was because someone had died. They were downsizing from large houses, and had to get rid of half the things they owned. One neighbor had so much, he held his own estate sale while he was still alive. Strange! But for Sunny, it had been the perfect move, at the perfect time in her life. She and Joe needed a fresh start after Marvin's death.

Sunny brought her train of thoughts back to the issue at hand. She knew she'd been mixing stuff up in her mind lately. Perhaps she was doing that this time, too. She really liked Nick. She thought he was a special kid. Well, he's not exactly a kid. Anyway, that was beside the point. She couldn't reconcile the Nick she knew, so warm and caring and Marvin-like, with that menacing figure at the theater.

What should she do? She knew she probably had enough information to go to the police, but was she jumping the gun? Was she pointing her finger at the wrong person? And where would that get her, or Nick? And would they believe her anyway, or just view her as a doddering old lady?

Sunny glanced at the clock. It was 6:30 AM, a respectable time to get the day started. As she'd gotten older, simple preparations for the day have become such a chore.

*If I did everything I was supposed to do to maintain myself at this age,* she thought, *I would be spending the whole day primping and on health-enhancing tasks. And even with that, it would be an uphill battle.*

Sunny laid out all her implements on the vanity sink. Front and foremost were a razor and shaving cream. Sunny remembered a story her grandmother used to tell about her own mother:

"My Mom was in the hospital on a women's ward." Sunny could almost hear her Granny's voice as she thought about it.

"I went to visit but couldn't find my Mom anywhere. I went by the beds two or three times, but I still didn't see her. Finally, I took a closer look at one woman. This woman looked like a man in the woman's ward. It was my mother. Her facial hair had grown in so much, she was unrecognizable. I was so distressed. I went home and made Grandpa and the kids promise that if I ever was in that situation, they'd be sure to shave me every day."

Sunny pulled a pair of black tapered pants, a comfortable t-shirt, and sensible shoes from the closet. She enjoyed getting dressed up for the special Regal Crest functions, the concerts, dinners and political meetings, but she especially liked that she no longer had to focus on what she was wearing on a day-to-day basis and could just be laid-back about it all. The only exception she made was baggy butts. That was really old lady-ish. She was on the fence though about old people going to the other extreme, trying to look stylish. That was a fine line! Sunny remembered seeing a woman who, from the back, looked so svelte and sexy, a man whistled in passing. But when he turned around, expecting youth and beauty, a pained look crossed his face instead. And then there was her neighbor, who wore modern, tight leggings with her walker.

Sunny brushed her hair, put on lipstick, and looked herself up and down in the mirror. *So, this is who I am. This is how I look at this time and place.*

*I wonder how Nick sees me when he sees me. Is he looking through me, or does he see me for the person I am? And what if that was him? What does that say about my ability to assess character? What if I went to the police and I was wrong? What would happen to Mae?*

Sunny went into the kitchen; and pulled out eggs, milk, butter and a small omelet pan. Marvin had loved the way she cooked eggs: fried, sunny-side up, and over-easy. She knew she was spoiling him. When he came home from breaks during college, or when he was living with them as a boomerang child, she would wake up each morning to make him breakfast, varying the side ingredients day to day: fried eggs with bacon and potatoes, with sausage and toast, with tomatoes and onions, on a bagel with cheese. She even went as far as putting it on a tray and serving him in bed when he was sleeping late. Marvin protested, but not really. He gleefully pulled himself up in bed, and thanked his mother profusely. He knew how to make sure she would do it again the next day. And Sunny loved doing this. It made her feel needed, and provided structure to the beginning of her day.

Sunny turned on the small kitchen television and tuned in to the local news. Across the bottom of the screen scrolled today's activities for Regal Crest: yoga class, drawing workshop, and political lecture. In the upper left-hand corner was a small window—the security camera that showed the front entrance and lobby. Sandwiched between the latest on the presidential race and the morning rush-hour traffic was a report on the theater bombing. There was a video clip of everyone loitering outside, stunned looks on their faces.

"There were no major injuries... police have found no motive... police have no leads. Anyone with any information, please call the emergency hotline that has been set up."

There were no injuries, and the police had no leads. That gave Sunny a window of opportunity. She knew what she was going to do. She was not going to go to the authorities until she explored more on her own.

Sunny was flooded with relief now that a decision had been made. Her mind flashed back to the Agatha Christie novels she used to read. She could fancy herself a Miss Marple. The first step was to gather information. She would start by dropping by Mae and Nick's early to catch them unaware.

# Chapter 11

# Nick

THE BRIGHT SUN seeped through the warped Venetian blinds. Nick flung his arm over his eyes and was about to turn on his side, but caught himself with a start. At the last minute, he remembered he was in his Grandma Mae's guest room, in a narrow twin bed. He reached for his cell phone. The electronic envelope icon was flashing. It was an email from Mike. He had followed up on Nick's phone call and was wasting no time. He was organizing a meeting for 9 AM this morning.

It was already 7:30 AM, and Nick was starting to feel the low-grade pain in his head re-intensify. His call to Mike was a knee-jerk reaction to his being laid off, on top of all of the tension of the day. He had mixed feelings about putting all of this in motion. Well, it was too late now.

Nick had stripped down to his underwear to sleep, so he pulled on a pair of wrinkled jeans and yesterday's t-shirt that he had left across the wooden side chair. He heard some movement beyond the door, and then a loud crash.

He stepped into his slippers and rushed outside. His grandmother Mae was standing in the kitchen, in the middle of a puddle of glass and remnants of a broken applesauce jar, and was walking around in her bare feet, preparing coffee.

"Be careful, grandma. You broke that jar."

"I did?" Mae looked down at her feet, incredulous. "Where did that come from? Where are my shoes?"

"Come, let me help you." Nick led Mae over to one of the vinyl kitchen chairs. He opened up the cabinet below the sink, and took out a kitchen towel and began to dry off Mae's feet. There was some blood and a few superficial scratches, but nothing serious. He opened the closet to get a broom and dustpan.

Mae sat on the chair, watching Nick. Tears brushed her eyes. "I'm hungry," she whispered.

Nick looked up at Mae's face. "Don't worry." He wiped one of Mae's tears away with the back of his hand. "I'll get you something to eat." He walked over to the refrigerator, but quickly turned around when he heard Mae shuffling behind him.

"I have to get ready to go to the museum," she said in an animated voice. " They are expecting me to help out with the school trip. The children like so much to put their hands in the touch-and-feel, and to pet the turtles and sea horses."

"No, grandma. You don't do that anymore."

Mae frowned. "I don't understand." She stood at the center of the room at a loss. "I think I'll go and watch TV." She took two steps toward the living room and stopped short. "Now what was it I was going to do?"

"Come, just sit down here." Nick went to the cabinet, took out a loaf of bread, and put one slice on a saucer and placed it in front of Mae. "I'll get some butter and jam." Nick went to the fridge and then turned around with the jars in his hand, but Mae had already finished the bread and was looking quizzically at the crumbs on her chest.

Nick sighed. He'd have to make sure Mae had more than that to eat, help her get dressed, and leave some food for her for lunchtime, and just in case he didn't get back on time, prepare dinner, too. And Mike was expecting him in less than an hour.

Nick turned on the small 12-inch TV on the kitchen counter. He remembered Mae being so excited that there was a cable outlet in the kitchen. "I've always wanted to be able to watch my favorite soap opera in the kitchen while I cook. Silly, I guess. But it makes me so happy." Mae was always so easy to please. Now her eyes were empty but glued to the screen, her chin slumped against her chest.

*The TV should keep her busy for a while*, Nick thought. He turned up the volume a bit so he could hear if there was any news about yesterday while he worked in the kitchen. It seemed the news anchors were already done with the serious news and had turned to fluff. Maybe he lucked out and the happenings at the movie theater would be a non-issue. After all, who really cared about a bunch of old people in a retirement community? That was part of the problem.

Nick reached down to the bottom shelf of the cabinet, pulled out a frying pan, and took some eggs and butter from the refrigerator. Mae already ate the bread. He would scramble some eggs, maybe slice some tomatoes on the side, mix in a can of tuna with the rest of the tomatoes for lunch. Then maybe he would hard-boil one of the eggs for a late afternoon snack, in case he was late for dinner. He hoped that should be simple enough for Mae to handle.

Nick had just dropped two eggs in a pot of water and had begun melting butter in the frying pan when the doorbell rang. Mae jumped with a start, but then slid back down in the kitchen chair again. Nick wiped his hands against the side of his jeans, reached over and gave Mae a soothing pat on her shoulder, and glanced at his watch. 8:30 AM. Who would be dropping by this early? For a minute, the thought flashed by that it might be someone for him… because of yesterday. But he was sure no one knew who he was. He had been careful. No one knew he was here. He was sure he was safe.

He opened the door. Sunny the landlady was there, holding a newspaper in her hand. Nick's heart lurched. The paper! Was there something in there that gave him away?

After all, Sunny knew he was at the scene yesterday. They had met outside.

"Oh, hi, Nick. Here's Mae's paper. It was left outside at the foot of the walkway. Lazy paperboy." Sunny handed it to Nick with the front page open. Nick quickly glanced at the headlines; there was nothing on the first page.

"Can I come in?" Sunny walked past Nick as she asked the question. Nick saw Sunny take a quick assessment of the kitchen as she walked towards Mae. The butter was browning and sizzling in the frying pan. Sunny reached over and turned off the flame. "How are you doing, Mae?"

Mae looked at Sunny with a blank stare, then remembered her manners. "Fine. And how are you?" It was clear she had no idea who she was talking to.

Sunny turned to Nick. "It looks like you have your hands full. This can't go on this way, you know."

Nick put his hands in his pocket and shrugged.

"Were you planning to go out? I'm free this morning. I can take it from here." Sunny took off her coat and threw it over an empty kitchen chair before settling into another one next to Mae. She took Mae's hand, but focused her gaze at Nick. "That was quite a happening last night. Did you get to work on time?"

Nick thought for a moment, and chose to ignore the first part of Sunny's statement and answer the second part. "It really didn't matter. The Breeze Café was empty, as usual. In fact, I was laid off. There weren't enough customers to justify keeping me on... and yes, I do have something to do this morning... was supposed to be there by nine o'clock.

"I have something to do, too," Mae said, mostly to herself. "If only I could remember what."

Sunny didn't miss a beat. "I'm sorry to hear that. What lousy luck," she said to Nick before turning her attention to Mae. "I'll help you get ready. After Nick leaves, I'll help you wash up and get dressed. That way, you'll be ready when you remember." Sunny could tell from the lost look in Mae's eyes that she was already on to something else.

"You don't mind?" Nick waved his hand around the kitchen and sighed.

"No, go ahead. I can stay until 12 or so. In fact, I'd like that... a long visit with Mae." Mae smiled as Sunny squeezed her hand again.

"Go ahead, get ready." Sunny looked at her watch. "It's almost nine now."

Nick walked into a small room off the kitchen. Sunny knew from the floor plans she used when renting condos that it was supposed to be a den, but most people used it as a guest room. Nick was probably using it as his bedroom. Mae was engrossed in a segment on TV on cooking breakfast burritos. Sunny cuddled close to her to give the impression of watching along, but in actuality her senses were tuned into what Nick was doing. Sunny heard a closet door open and close, the squeak of a cabinet hinge, water running, a toilet flushing—that would be the half-bath—then she heard the ubiquitous musical notes as a computer was turned on, followed by the clicking of the keyboard.

It was 8:56. Nick signed into his email account to check Mike's message for where the meeting was being held. Shit. It was on the other side of town. He'd better hurry. He jumped up from the computer, slipped on his sneakers, and pulled on his navy hoodie as he rushed out the room.

"Thanks again, Sunny." He turned to Mae. 'Have a good day, grandma."

Sunny waited a good five minutes after hearing the door slam behind Nick before extricating herself from Mae on the pretense of taking the dishes into the kitchen. Instead, she slipped into the den. She was sure she hadn't heard the telltale melody of the computer closing. Just as she thought, in his rush, Nick had left the computer open to the page he was reading.

She quickly glanced over the screen.

To: Nick
From: Mike
Subject: Re: This IS The Plan.

# Chapter 12

# Sunny

Sunny inhaled a quick, sharp breath. Clearly, something was going on, and it was beyond just Nick. Sunny walked back to the doorway and glanced into the kitchen. Mae was still hunched over the breakfast table. She didn't seem to know that Sunny was gone.

She headed back into Nick's room, and quickly scanned and scrolled through the open email on the computer. There was nothing more than a sentence or two about a meeting this morning. This email must be part of a thread called Re: This IS The Plan. *It will take a while for me to figure that out. I'll have to find a way to get back to the computer before Nick gets back.*

For now, Sunny memorized the meeting location, and then looked about her. The room was sparsely furnished: it had just a closet, a narrow bed, a side table, a chair, a child-sized desk, a small TV, and a four-drawer dresser. She glanced at the entryway again. Mae was still occupied. She quietly slipped open the drawer of the night table and rummaged around inside: a pack of gum, a set of keys, a bottle opener, a note pad and pen—nothing unusual here. She did the same thing with the dresser drawer. She inched down her hands and knees and looked under the bed. There was a plastic sweater box, but it was empty.

Sunny glanced out at the kitchen again before heading to the closet. Mae had changed her position in her chair, but was still focused on the TV. Sunny turned the knob of the closet door and was able to open it quietly. Inside hung a wardrobe of hoodies in steel-gray, black, and tan. Next to them were two pairs of jeans, one brown corduroy slacks, and a pair of khakis. Two pairs of scuffed sneakers were tossed onto the floor.

Sunny was just about to close the door when she noticed a shiny glint in the back corner. She pushed the clothing aside. Inside, leaning against the far back corner, was a rifle. Next to it was an army-green canvas bag, its drawstring closure tightly drawn and triple-knotted.

Sunny stepped back with a start and stared into the dark corner. What was she expecting when she started this search? Hadn't she been expecting something like this? But the guy in the movie theater hadn't had a rifle. It would have been too big and cumbersome, and made it difficult to manipulate the smoke bomb. And didn't men keep rifles on hand for hunting? He probably put it back here for safekeeping. But why would Nick have brought this along to just temporarily stay at Mae's? And the bag? What was in the bag?

Sunny looked behind her again before getting on her hands and knees and crawling along the bottom of the closet. She pulled the canvas bag out and squatted as she worked on undoing the knot. Inside were two handguns and an assortment of magazine clips. Instinctively, Sunny reached in to pull one out, to feel the cold metal and the weight against her hands, but stopped herself in time. Fingerprints! The lessons of all those detective books she enjoyed reading were not lost on her.

Sunny's legs were beginning to cramp. She sat back on her heels and began retying the knot. Darn! She should have made a mental note of how it was tied before she untied it. She was so focused on this task that she didn't hear Mae enter the room.

"Gun. Nick's gun."

Sunny jumped up with a start, simultaneously kicking the bag against the back-closet wall. She could hear the bag hitting the rifle and the rifle sliding down against the sidewall. There was nothing she could do about that now. Sunny took a quick yogic breath, and tried to calm herself before turning around to face Mae. Her heart was racing, but she made sure to have a calm and serene look on her face and a half-smile on her lips. Mae would forget this moment in a few minutes.

"Oh, there you are, Mae. Finished watching TV? Let's plan what we are going to do this morning." Sunny took Mae's elbow and led her out the room.

Mae followed Sunny, but kept turning her head to look behind her. "I just don't understand," she muttered, and gave Sunny an angry look.

Thirty minutes later, Sunny had gotten Mae fed and dressed and settled in a chair by the window, where she could watch the morning activities of Regal Crest. Most importantly, between washing dishes and buttoning and snapping, she had formulated a plan. But first, she'd have to take a closer look at what was on Nick's computer.

Sunny slipped back into the den and pushed a key on Nick's computer. The screen brightened up as it left sleep mode. The email from someone named Mike was still open. Sunny sat in the swivel desk chair and took her time to carefully read it. *Someone has to stop this before it gets started*, she thought.

Sunny glanced around her. Mae was shifting restlessly in her chair. She only had a few minutes. Although Mae would probably forget, she didn't want to take a chance on her spending this much time in Nick's room being filed somewhere in Mae's brain to come out later.

She quickly forwarded Mike's letter to her own email account, and then had another idea. She searched Nick's hard drive for anything with Mike's name. Two other items came up, and she attached those to an email to herself, too.

She sat back for a minute, feeling very proud that she had figured out how to do this so quickly. Sunny, like many people her age, was computer-challenged. Thank God she had attended that beginner's computer class offered by the Apple Club in Clubhouse 2.

Chapter 13

# Mike

MIKE PUSHED THE night button on the door of the square warehouse building located on the edge of 7th Street. The meeting would be held in the conference room of a shipping company a friend had started with the remnants of his 401k after work had dried up—if you could call the room stacked with inventory and old machinery a conference room. It was far enough away from the center of things, but near a bus stop—a necessity these days, given that many of his contemporaries could no longer afford a car.

It was early. The sky was just beginning to glow orange and purple beyond the skyline. Mike wanted to give himself time to set things up and just sit and think.

Finally, the night watchman came and opened the door. It was clear from the creases on his face that he had been sleeping—probably with his cheek leaning against the upholstered back of a chair. He had a bored, 'is this all there is to life' look on his face. He was Mike's target audience. Mike rustled through his bag and pulled out a handout.

"Hey, What time do you get off? There's a meeting in the basement you might be interested in at 9." He stuffed the flyer in the night watchman's hand.

The elevator was right at the entrance, but Mike went down the stairway instead. *Might as well get the lay of the land now*, he thought. Ever since he started on this project, he'd been thinking in these doomsday ways. It never hurt to be too careful.

There was a lot of work to do in the room, starting with setting up tables and chairs. He was expecting 12 people, including Nick: a core group to work with. He decided to bunch the tables in the middle of the room to make a large square, and put the chairs around them. That way, they could all see each other when talking—it would help with the bonding process. Mike remembered that tip from some psychology book he read. There was nothing he could do about all the odds and ends around the room. Maybe it was better, though. It gave the room a secretive, eerie feeling.

When he was finished, it was almost 8 o'clock—almost an hour to the meeting, enough time to get some coffee and donuts. People always appreciated getting something for free, and having something to eat for some would mean they wouldn't have to spend money on breakfast or lunch later. It would mean he would have to part with a much-needed twenty-dollar bill. Perhaps he could cut the donuts in half and buy just 6 instead of 12. Mike had already laid out money for making copies, and he was using up all of the allotted minutes on his cell phone. He'd have to find a way to get the others to chip in if they were going to continue with meetings like this in the future.

When Mike returned at 8:30 AM, a cardboard coffee caddy in one hand and a greasy paper bag in the other, there were already two men sitting in the room. Each had taken a seat at the opposite end of the table from each other. One was hunched over a copy of the free local paper, pen in hand, probably doing a crossword puzzle or Sudoku. The other was fiddling with his cell phone. Mike didn't recognize either one of them. In fact, he only directly knew a few people who were coming. The rest were acquaintances or friends of friends.

This is the part Mike hated the most: small talk and getting-to-know-you. Sure, he looked like an out-there person, but deep down he was still the quiet, introverted, kid he had been for the first sixteen years of his life.

"Hi there. Glad you could make it. I'm Mike. I have some coffee and donuts here." Mike placed the snacks at the end of the table. He was too embarrassed to cut the donuts now with people watching. The latecomers won't know how many there were initially. They'll think they just missed out.

# Chapter 14

# Sunny

Sunny climbed out the taxi a block away from the meeting location, and reached around to help Mae take off her seatbelt and get out the door. It was an impulsive decision to come here. It now seemed like the stupidest thing to do. And what about Mae? She should have left her home alone, or with a neighbor. Nick did that all the time. She wasn't thinking clearly. But this was too important. Anyway, it was too late now.

Sunny waited until the Walk sign came on, then began crossing the street. People heading in their direction smiled at them. They probably looked like an old mother and her aging caretaker daughter. How cute. They barely had enough time to make it to the other side before the number countdown stopped.

Sunny didn't have to refer to the address. She had burned it in her brain, as she could have as easily forgotten it. A few steps around the corner and they would be there.

The entrance to the boxy building did not have a wheelchair button, and the door was hard for Sunny to pull open. She held it long enough for them to slip through and then let it slam shut. The meeting was in room A-1. That would probably be on the first floor, or in the basement.

Sunny checked the numbers on the first floor, then took the elevator down one flight. She could hear loud voices as they entered the hallway.

She put her fingers to her lips. "Shhhh!" she motioned to Mae. Mae put her fingers to her lips too and smiled, her eyes gleaming as if she were enjoying this secret expedition.

Sunny walked quietly to the meeting room and pulled the door open a crack. She could see the men sitting and talking. There was a pile of boxes and a stack of folding chairs by the side of the entrance. If she and Mae could slip behind them, it would be a good vantage point to see what was going on.

Sunny took Mae's hand and led her in that direction, continuing to signal with her free hand for Mae to be quiet. She motioned to Mae to stand silently and attempted to unfold two chairs. As she pulled the seat down on the second one, the metal legs scrapped along the floor, making a low screeching noise. A man in a three-piece suit and a man with full arm tattoos sitting next to him both turned to look in their direction for a few seconds, then turned back.

"Whew! That was close."

Sunny waved Mae toward one of the seats, sat down next to her, then took Mae's hand in hers. A few minutes later, she could feel Mae's body shaking as a giggle made its way through her body. Sunny held her breath, her mind racing trying to figure out a way to stop her.

"Fun!" Mae laughed. The resonating sound was thankfully drowned out by a loud and heated argument that erupted among the men at the table at the same moment.

# Chapter 15

# Mike

Mike pulled out his cell phone and pushed the "on" button. 9:05. He ran his fingers over the smooth glass screen. Cell phones: a simple example of the divide between the older and younger generations. Older people wear watches.

Mike had just read an article about how phone thieves were trying to get around this problem. Cell phone users knew the dangers of using them on the streets or on the subway, so they kept them hidden. But if someone came up and asked them for the time, their politeness gene kicked in and they reached for their phone to check the time. Once the phone was out in the open, the thief snatched it and ran off. It's very simple but ingenious, if you think about it. Their group needed to be as creative with their plan.

Mike looked down again. 9:13. Mike willed Nick to walk through the door. He would be much better at running the meeting and explaining The Plan. But he couldn't wait any longer. Eleven men were sitting around the table expectantly, and he could see they were getting restless.

"Hello. I guess we should get started. Thank you for coming. My name is Mike." Eleven pairs of eyes turned to stare at him. For a minute, Mike felt himself turn inward, like his old self, the nerdy kid in high school. But then he remembered his persona, his look, his tight arm muscles and tattoos.

He pulled himself up straighter.

"Does everyone have a handout?" There were nods around the table and the rustle of paper as people reached for the sheet in front of them.

"Then you know why we're here. We're here to take control of our lives. We're here to stabilize our future. We're here to balance the scales between us and the older generation."

Mike knew he wasn't President Obama in his speaking style, but he did expect some response. He paused for a minute. There was a tentative clap by a man in a faded denim cap, but no one joined in. Mike turned his head slightly, letting his eyes rest slowly on each man sitting around the table, and let out an internal sigh that he hoped only he could hear.

"Let's take a minute to introduce ourselves to each other. Why don't you begin?" Mike turned to the man who had clapped. He hesitated but then stood up, took off his cap, and wrung it in his hands as he talked.

"My name is Wilfred, but people call me Bill. My story is probably not much different from the rest of you. There's no work out there. I've tried everything, even going to training programs to be a computer specialist, to be an EMT, to be a nurse's aide. Everyone tells me I'm good at what I do, but then no one wants to hire me. I've gone on more interviews. Sometimes, I get called back two or three times, but then it's a 'no go'. The unemployment has run out. I just don't know where to go from here. All I know is that what you are saying makes sense. Maybe we shouldn't make the older generation the scapegoat. I love my Mom and Dad. But everything worked right for them. I want some of that for me."

This time, there was clapping all around the table as Bill gave a tentative smile and took his seat. *That's an encouraging sign*, Mike thought. *It means they are ready to support each other. They are beginning to bond.*

Right away, another man stood up. He had a gaunt face and a wiry frame. The checkered shirt he wore with a thin tie hung off of his shoulders. A wide belt around his waist cinched baggy pants. Mike wondered for a moment if he was getting enough to eat, or maybe he'd been sick.

"Hi! My name is James." He paused for a moment. "Hi, James," came the response from the group.

Mike was surprised. Just a few minutes ago, they barely reacted to his rah-rah speech. He was amazed at how quickly they were warming up. It was beginning to feel like an AA meeting.

"I'm wearing this tie and will be leaving shortly because I have a go-see with a department head at the university downtown. I'm a researcher by training, but like Bill, I haven't been able to get any work. I've been losing weight. I look in the mirror. I know my appearance is strange. I don't know if it's the worry, the meatless meals, or something scary, but it doesn't help when I try to sell myself to the public. I wish I had some kind of medical coverage like the seniors have Medicare. I'd go to the doctor to make sure nothing's wrong."

Two people clamored to be the next ones to speak: Steve, followed by Frank. The story was the same one over and over again, just framed differently.

John was the last person to talk. His voice had a low timber; and he stretched out his vowels like a preacher would, giving his words a staccato beat. He was perfect to give the final introduction. His style of talking contributed to the buzz and excitement that was growing in the room.

Mike was half-listening—all the introductions blended together. Instead, his mind was shooting ahead to how he would manage the crowd when John stopped talking. Mike was good as the back-office person—the one to make things happen. But could he handle being up front and center? Would he be able to harness the energy and take it to the next level? No way. If only Nick were here.

Just as that thought crossed his mind, the door opened, and Nick rushed in. Mike didn't realize how worried he was about whether or not Nick would show up until relief whooshed out of his body like a deflated balloon. Now he could just relax and watch the magic happen.

# Chapter 16

# Nick

O**N HIS WAY** to the meeting, Nick thought about different scenarios and how things would go. He imagined stepping through the door and the room being empty, or finding Mike trying to make small talk with one or two people. Now, right outside the meeting room, he opened the door a crack and looked in. There was Mike sitting tall. Mike seemed to be in control, but Nick could see below the surface. There was a deer-in-the-headlight look about him. The room took on an energy of its own as a dynamic speaker raised his fist in the air before sitting down.

Never for a minute did he imagine that this many people would show up. In fact, he realized now, he was hoping they wouldn't.

Nick felt tightness across his forehead and lifted his arm to massage his temple. For the umpteenth time, he thought, *What have I gotten myself into?* Well, it was too late now.

Nick closed the door quietly so no one would hear him. He would be expected to be hurrying and out of breath, coming to the meeting so late. He stepped back to the other end of the hallway and gave himself a running start, propelling his body through the door into the room, making a huge staccato sound. Everyone turned in his direction.

"Hi. Sorry I'm so late. I'm Nick, the Mastermind." Nick paused a few seconds until he heard a small chuckle and then let his lips curl into a strange smile. "Thanks, Mike, for getting things started. I see you are just about done with introductions. Let me tell you a bit about myself."

This part was easy for Nick. He liked talking about himself. But at the same time, he could feel his mind split in two. That seemed to be happening more often lately. He could see and hear himself talking, but at the same time, another dialogue was going on in his head, like this one saying, "What's going on right now?"

"And I just lost the dead-end job I had," Nick heard Nick saying. "It felt like the last straw for me. It was a dinky job at a café, and I couldn't even keep that. It seems like it's getting harder and harder to survive.

"Did you hear about the bombing at the Regal Crest Shopping Plaza? I work near the theater and I was there, waiting for my shift to begin, when the bomb went off. Whoever did that did us a favor."

*I'm boasting,* the second half of Nick's mind thought. *Be careful.*

"You should have seen how scared those old people were, like they've never had a real problem in their lives. Sure, some of them lived through WWII, the Holocaust. Do you think they remember that now? It's ancient history. Lately, everything is so easy for them.

"We have to focus on the way things are at this moment, and it's simple. They control and are profiting from the money, jobs, income streams, and benefits; and we are left with nothing. Want to know where all our problems stem from? The buck stops here: right at the feet of people who are 70, 80 and 90 years old, such as those who live at Regal Crest.

And the reason why I think the movie bomber did us a favor…"

*There you go again,* Nick said to Nick. *You're full of yourself, aren't you?*

"…is the realization that we can begin implementation here—putting the plan in place a step at a time. Our county can be the prototype for the nation.

"No one really seems to care. That's understandable. Old people with one foot out the door aren't important. There was only a small mention of the theater incident in the paper, a 30-second clip on TV, and as far as I know, no follow-up.

We'd be under the radar. This would be the perfect place to start."

Nick looked around the table. Everyone seemed to be tuned in except for one man, in a gold and orange Mega Supermarket employee t-shirt, who was half-asleep on a propped-up elbow. Mike was nodding, a satisfied look on his face.

"Any questions?"

A thick, hairy arm cuffed by a rolled-up work shirt shot in the air.

"Yes. Your name, please."

"Mitch."

"Go on, Mitch."

"I was just wondering…" Mitch began tentatively. "You say it's a perfect place to start. Start what? And how? What exactly are we going to do? You applaud the theater bomber as if violence is the model. Is that what you mean?"

"It's too much to discuss in a short meeting. We'll go over the details another time. Just try to think about things broadly." Nick was exasperated, and this was only the first question. He hoped his impatience didn't show.

"It would be better to think about it as tough love, when you treat people harshly with the intent of helping in the long run," Nick continued. "Our goal is to accomplish something for the good of all. That makes it alright."

"I don't know how I feel about that," said the man in denim overalls, who had his straight and long black hair pulled back in a ponytail.

"Yeah, me too," another chimed in.

A buzz broke out among the men.

At that moment, there was a scraping noise and a girlish voice from the back of the room. Two men turned toward the direction of the sounds, as did Nick. They listened closely and shrugged.

Before turning his head back to the meeting, Nick saw a flash of pink cotton eyelet fabric that reminded him of the material in a dress that Mae owned. He gave his eyes a couple of strong blinks and looked again. Nothing. He tapped his forehead and rubbed his temple. It was natural to think about Mae and how this would impact her life, but having these hallucinations didn't help. He'd have to be strong.

# Chapter 17

# Sunny

Mae's hand was cold; Sunny's was warm and sweaty. Sunny tightened her grip around Mae's fingers. The physical contact might keep Mae calm and remind her that she was here with her and was safe.

Despite the situation, Sunny's body drew in the physicality of the connection. *It is so easy to take something like hand-holding for granted*, Sunny thought. She didn't realize how important these little displays of affection were until Joe was gone, and the possibility was no longer there. She missed the skin-to-skin contact and closeness.

No wonder Sunny's palms were damp. She couldn't remember the last time she had been this nervous. It was bad enough just being here, hiding in the corner, but trying to keep Mae quiet was adding a lot of stress to the situation.

Mae was squirming in her chair, her face scrunched up with a quizzical expression. "That's Nick. I hear Nick," she said in a low voice. "Hi, Nick!" she started to say loudly, but stopped herself when Sunny, again, put her finger to her lips. An angry look flashed across Mae's face. Then her affect went blank as she sat stiffly, just looking ahead. *She's lost the moment*, Sunny guessed, glad to have a minute to focus elsewhere.

Sunny looked out at the meeting beyond the stack of boxes. The loud disagreements seemed to have died down, and Nick had the floor again. Sunny could barely make out the words; she refused to wear a hearing aid, but she could tell he was animated in what he was saying. She strained to listen.

"Right now, this may seem more theoretical than practical. But trust me, things will start rolling along once we've put all the pieces in place." Nick was pacing and punctuating the air with his arms as he lectured.

"It's very simple. The main thing is to understand and buy into the concept. We all agree that the last 20 years of life—for those who make it beyond 70—are a total waste and drain on our society. With this plan, billions would be saved on medical care, caretakers, and retirement homes. Assets would be freed up for millennials; pensions would be more robust as they could be stretched to serve a smaller population. People would still retire at 65, but would only be on the Social Security rolls for five years instead of 25.

"Rather than worrying at retirement how they will make it financially for the next 25 years, seniors would focus on the first five years: golden, quality years. At 65, in addition to starting Social Security payments, the government would give everyone a $30,000 bonus to be used for travel or whatever else is on one's bucket list. That's less than the average two-year payment of Social Security and the individual experience it would help support would be more fun than working at Walmart, hunched over, greeting customers into the dreary future. At 70, seniors would plan a beautiful, golden ceremony involving children, grandchildren, friends, relatives and co-workers: a landmark celebration similar to weddings, christenings and yes, funerals: a punctuation to a rich, full life.

"Think about the people you know who are over 70. I bet they are struggling with their finances, health, or their mental state. They look in the mirror every morning, only to see more wrinkles, twitching, sagging skin, big ears, thinning hair. Every day, they physically move further and further away from the mainstream of our youth-oriented society.

"Now, think of the alternative I'm proposing: a full, rich life for all. Wouldn't you rather have 70 quality years than 100 years, with the last third of your life going down the toilet?" Nick paused for a few seconds, but not long enough for someone to actually give an answer. "Sure, we are giving up longevity, but the rest of our lives will be guaranteed perfection: solid and financially robust."

Nick paused. Everyone was just sitting in a catatonic state. Finally, a chair scraped as the tattooed man stood. He put his hands together and began a long, drawn-out clapping. One by one, the others in the room followed until they were all up on their feet clapping, hooting and engaging each other in discussions.

Nick put his head down, just long enough to erase the self-satisfied look that he could feel was crossing his face. He had to remember this wasn't all about him. "Thanks. Thanks for your support... Thanks. Now, let's get started."

Sunny had almost forgotten where she was, or that she was here with Mae. Her stomach curled. It sounds like... She covered her mouth quickly, sure she was going to throw up. Fortunately, those were just dry, silent heaves.

Remembering Mae, Sunny quickly looked over her shoulder and was struck by the serene, peaceful look on Mae's face and her curious, kid-like smile as her wrinkled fingers tried to play with the dust particles visible in the few tiny streams of sunlight that filtered in the room through narrow windows.

Chapter 18

# Sunny

Sunny felt a deep, gnawing pain beginning to make its way up her body, and a sharp wave of envy as she looked over at Mae. Just for a moment, she wanted to be Mae right now—to have no awareness of what was going on, to not have heard the plans. And Nick… why Nick?

Without thinking, Sunny put her hands over her ears and rocked her head from side to side.

Mae looked over from the dust particles and watched Sunny. A smile spread across her face.

"Games. Hear no evil, speak no evil, see no evil… hear no evil, speak no evil, see no evil." Mae chanted over and over, quickening her pace, her voice getting louder. "Monkey. Monkey." She moved her wrinkled fingers first over her ears, then her mouth, then her eyes, continuing in frenzy. "Hear no… speak no…"

"Shhhh." Sunny put her fingers to her lips, admonishing Mae.

"Hear no evil, speak no evil, see no evil. Monkey. Monkey," Mae rebelliously whispered in a low, hoarse voice as she flapped her hands around before collapsing onto herself, her chin on her chest, a few drops of drool escaping the corner of her mouth.

Sunny looked out into the meeting. No one seemed to have heard Mae. The men were still talking loud and animatedly among themselves. That was a close call. It was time to get out of here before Mae gave them away. Sunny had heard more than enough, anyway. It was more than she ever wanted to know.

Sunny leaned over and reached for Mae's hand. Mae took it willingly, an empty look on her face as her eyes moved around. Suddenly, a flash of recognition appeared. "What a nice place. Are you moving?" Mae scanned the boxes piled up around them.

Sunny was quick with her response. "Yes, I'm moving after all these years. I just wanted you to see the house one last time. We can go now."

Sunny walked slowly so she could maneuver Mae carefully through the narrow pathway that led to the back door. Mae dragged her feet as she walked. Sunny hadn't noticed that shuffling before. It sounded so loud now, but she could hear the din of the loud talking and clapping still going on in the background, so maybe it was okay.

There were a few feet from where they would be exposed before they got to the door. Sunny glanced over her shoulder one last time and quickly maneuvered Mae across that area, pressing them both against the door jam. She quietly opened the door and slipped through, only to see a broad form moving quickly ahead of them.

She pulled Mae to the side, and they again flattened their backs, pressing into the wall. Instinctively, forgetting what happened previously, Sunny put her fingers across her lips to motion Mae to keep silent. Mae opened her mouth to protest but, in that moment, there was a crescendo of clapping in the room behind them that caused Mae to lose her train of thought. She closed her mouth, her eyes glazing over again.

The increase in sound volume caused the man walking in front of them to momentarily turn in their direction, but his focus was on the men's room, his hand clutching his crotch. Sunny and Mae headed around the corner to the waiting elevator, and through the front door onto the main level and out into the broad sunshine, without being seen.

Sunny tried not to rush Mae, but suddenly it seemed very important to get as far away from here as quickly as possible. It would be better to walk by the closest bus stop and wait at the one closer to the Ryton Mall. There would be more people there. It was too early for lunch, but those on an early shift were already loitering around.

There was a small space on the bench at the kiosk. Sunny positioned herself and Mae right in front of the young people sitting down, but none of them made an attempt to move over. Instead, they sat firm with their legs splayed, staring into their smart phones.

"Excuse me," Sunny growled and spread her hands in a move-over motion to show what she expected them to do. One boy looked up and glanced at his cell phone again, but then hauled himself off the bench, using his free hand to tug on his pants as they slipped down below his waist. He went over to the frame of the kiosk, leaned his weight against the side, and went back to his phone. Now if Sunny could just get the young girl to slide over slightly, there would be room for her and Mae.

A half-hour later, they were back at Mae's villa. Sunny felt a stream of tension rush out of her body as she crossed the apartment threshold. They were back at Regal Crest, and it felt safe.

Sunny sat Mae down at the kitchen table. Mae did a good job making it all the way home, but the trip seemed to have taken a toll on her. She sat there, just staring ahead, her hands folded on the table. Sunny could tell Mae was very tired. Her face was pale and seemed more wrinkled. Her forehead was sweaty, and there was spittle in the corner of her mouth. Sunny went and wet a paper towel, and wiped it across Mae's face. *Nick would be very upset if he knew I went traipsing off with his grandmother today*, Sunny thought before remembering. *No, Nick wouldn't care at all!*

*What's up with Nick?*

Sunny's mind began to puzzle over the events of the morning as she went to the sink to fill the kettle and make some tea. She noticed the empty Tupperware containers stacked up in the sink, each labeled breakfast, lunch and dinner. There was so much evidence of Nick's caring: the food preparation, the notes on the refrigerator door.

"If Marvin hadn't died, he would have been around to do this for me one day." A sole tear trickled out of the corner of Sunny's eye. She wiped her face with the back of her hand. She found herself getting emotional often and so unexpectedly as she got older.

Mae looked over at Sunny's face with a question mark on her mind. "Sad?" She pushed her chair back, using the armrests to raise herself up, shuffled over to the stove where Sunny was standing, and gave her a hug. Sunny was caught off-guard but smiled, took Mae's elbow and led her back to the table. She went to the stove and returned again with the hot cups of tea. Mae sat with her fingers knitted around the cup. Sunny could tell from the peaceful expression on her face that Mae was already in another place.

A wave of jealousy passed over Sunny again. It was stupid to be envious of someone who had dementia and no short-term memory, and yet there was something to be said about being able to forget what she heard this morning. Sunny's mind never rested: it was always problem-solving, always trying to find a solution, always trying to figure something out. And when faced with something like this, it was almost painful as explosions of thoughts and ideas took over.

Sunny sighed and glanced at her watch. She didn't want to be here when Nick returned. Perhaps she should put Mae in her pajamas—she was probably due for a nap. In fact, they both were. Sunny wished she could just crawl in right behind Mae and pull the covers up to her chin.

It took twenty minutes for Sunny to get Mae settled and tucked into bed. Mae laid there, her white hair splayed across the pillow, looking up at Sunny who was sitting on the high ladder-back chair at her side. Her eyes closed and opened as her breathing got slower and shallower. Her face softened. Finally, she was asleep.

The room was silent and peaceful. Sunny's heart opened. She remembered quiet moments like this when Marvin was a baby as she sat by his side, marveling at his soft breath and his little lungs going up and down, up and down. In those spaces of time, all felt right with the world. Sunny felt a sweet maternal urge as she watched Mae. Her body relaxed into the feeling, only to snap into rigidity as she remembered: nothing was right with the world now. In fact, it was all very wrong.

# Chapter 19

# Mike

Mike looked around him. The growing crescendo of clapping was making his head throb. He felt on edge and wound up. This would be a good time to go out and have a long-awaited pee.

The men's room was empty, but out of habit, he headed over to the urinal at the farthest end for some semblance of privacy. He held his penis lightly. What a relief! He could feel the tension subside as the urine streamed out with a steady whoosh. He shook his member, and unconsciously his hand began to tighten. He pulled on his organ. His breath began to quicken, bringing awareness to what he was doing. He dropped his hand down and rubbed the side of his jeans. Did it still come to this? Jerking off to relieve stress was a habit he got into in high school.

Mike quickly zipped up his pants, walked over to the sink, and scrubbed his hands. He looked at his face in the mirror and was comforted by what he saw. The edges of green and black tattoos creeping up along his neck reminded him that he was no longer the Mikey of his school days.

Mike turned his mind to what had just happened at the meeting. Had he gotten himself roped into Nick's plans tighter than he thought? What he just heard was scary. Nick was taking this further than he ever imagined. Had he misunderstood Nick? Was the idea to actually kill people off? He thought they were just isolating them. If this was truly the case, this was a new ballgame. Too much! But…was he locked into these plans? After all, he was now seen as one of the leaders. A cowardly leader (as only he knew), but a leader nevertheless.

Mike's stomach began to lurch as his mind raced. He could feel the bitter vomit at the bottom of his throat; and he leaned over the sink, retching. He wiped off his mouth with the back of his hand and caught his eyes in the mirror again, staring himself down.

*Pull yourself together!* Mike realized he was a bit jealous of Nick. Perhaps that was coloring his perspective. How easy it was for Nick to be out there, spinning a yarn and captivating an audience. Mike was just grateful he was in here, if only for a brief respite, and didn't have to high–five and small-talk and whoop it up with everyone. Anyway, what did it matter at the end of the day, as long as he was able to do his part and get things done?

When Mike returned, he saw a frustrated Nick at the front of the room, still trying to pull the group back to order. Nick nodded his way, signaling that Mike should join him. But Mike averted his eyes, pretending he didn't see.

"OK, everyone. We only have a few minutes left. Let's get going on our plans. There are two things that still need to be done." Nick held up a blank sheet of paper. "I need everyone to give me his name and email. By doing this, you also agree that you'll keep this confidential for the time being. We'll keep the group small, at 13, until we flesh out our plans more." Nick put the paper on the table by the patched elbow of the man sitting closest to him. "Any questions?" Nick's eyes scanned the room, and again he tried to make eye contact with Mike, but Mike had snapped his head down.

"Next, think about someone close to you who is over 70. Think about who they are. Think about what their life is like. See how it feels to be them. Immerse yourself in this person mentally, and bring him or her in your mind to our next meeting as a virtual test case."

Mike felt queasy again. The idea was so repulsive. Yet he was surprised that automatically, he had started sifting through possible candidates in his mind like a Rolodex.

"There's a higher purpose," Nick chanted over the other chatter in his head. "There's an important reason to get this done."

Mike carefully lifted his head to look up to see how the other men were reacting, only to stare into Nick's face, whose gaze had remained on him, waiting to lock in with what Mike saw now as a sickly smile on his face.

# Chapter 20

# Sunny

Sunny tiptoed out of Mae's bedroom, quietly closing the door behind her. She looked around for her purse and sweater, and noticed the door to Nick's room was ajar. She was tempted to go back in and nose around some more, but what else could she find? She had enough snooping for one day. It was more important for her to be long gone before Nick got back home.

Besides, she always had an excuse to return here: Mae's condition. She'd have to incorporate that in her plan when she came up with one. And she'd have to do something about Mae. Her real-estate property wasn't safe with Mae living here as it was.

Sunny remembered when a resident had left a boiling pot of water on the stove one night, a few days after she and Joe moved to Regal Crest. They were awakened in the middle of the night by a piercing siren and flashing lights. The smoke detector and fire alarms had been activated.

Sunny threw her bathrobe over her pajamas. Joe pulled on a pair of jeans under his sleep shirt, and they headed down the stairs to the front of the building. That is how they met their neighbors: while wearing a blue-and-pink bathrobe, a plaid nightshirt, and house slippers. Women with tight pin curls or fabric curlers stood next to men in navy cotton pajamas. It took a while for Sunny not to think of their nighttime attire when she saw her neighbors on the street.

* * *

Sunny worried about what would happen to Mae when she woke up and Nick wasn't there. How would she manage when she couldn't even follow a chain of thought? But Nick left her alone all the time, and nothing had happened so far. What Sunny wasn't aware of, she could do nothing about. She'd just have to keep her fingers crossed.

Marvin used to tease her about just this. He would come to spend a few days in the second bedroom of his parents' condo and go out for the night with his buddies, often not returning until two or three in the morning. Sunny couldn't go to bed until he was home safe and sound.

Marvin would just shake his head when he got home and found his Mom slumped in a kitchen chair, snoozing at the corner table that was placed by the window. "But mom, what about all the days I'm not here with you? You don't know what I'm doing. You have no way of knowing if you should be worrying or not." Sunny would just smile and laugh, but more from relief that he was back safe and sound than from the irony of the situation.

Sunny took one last look around Mae's apartment before heading out the door. The salmon-colored carpet and the ornate beige-and-green wallpaper of the hallway closed in around her. The interiors of the buildings were due for a renovation. She'd have to remember to bring this up at the condo's board meeting. Perhaps they could redo it to something more contemporary. The baby boomers who were starting to move in liked their surroundings to be more modern than what was possible with gold and flock.

Sunny exited through the back of the apartment complex. She took a deep breath of fresh, clean air. The campus was beautifully landscaped. Purple and yellow peonies were sprinkled among dark-green ferns on one side of the walkway and raspberry-colored flowers blooming from low hedges lined the other. A rabbit scampered through the underbrush; a Delmarva fox squirrel scurried up a tree.

Sunny took the footbridge to Regal Crest Boulevard and arrived at Clubhouse I just in time to catch the on-site shuttle bus back home.

"Hi, Bess." Sunny smiled at her favorite bus driver, a caring middle-aged woman with an infectious laugh, and then shifted her focus to concentrate on pulling herself onto the high, deep-set bottom step of the Regal Crest bus using both side handrails.

Surprisingly, given the people who live here, the design of this bus wasn't elderly-friendly at all, especially for the many people who tried to navigate it with walkers and more Mega Supermarket shopping bags then they could realistically manage. A group of residents had tried to get the directors of Regal Crest Corporation to apply some of the money that had been set aside for the Facility Enhancement Fund to an updated and accessible bus, but to no avail. *They'd rather spend the money on stupid renovations like putting up mirrored walls in the ballroom*, Sunny thought.

She nodded to the other people on the bus and edged herself into the seat behind the driver.

"Haven't seen you for a while, Sunny." Bess had a photographic memory and easily remembered everyone's name and their drop-off points. It felt special to be called by name, especially for people who no longer had someone to greet them in their lives. In fact, some people rode the bus just so they would have someone to talk to in a given day.

"Is everything okay? What have you been doing?"

Sunny's mind froze. All she could remember was the meeting this morning. For a brief moment, Sunny thought perhaps she could talk about what she had seen and heard with Bess. She could almost anticipate her calming words, her concerned cooing, her questions, her "Well, dear, I wouldn't take that seriously," or her high laughter as she tossed if off as unimportant. Or perhaps Bess would take it seriously and make one of her famous analogies. Even that would be comforting. But the minute that idea crossed her mind and almost slipped out of her mouth, she knew she had to strangle it. This was something she'd have to keep to herself, at least for now.

"I've been busy, I guess. Although I don't know why, given that I'm retired."

"It does seem like there's always so much to do," a man in the back seat chipped in. "The bill-paying, doctor's appointments, volunteer work, grandchildren. I feel busier than when I was working as a project manager for the federal government, and yet back then, I was doing all this and working, too."

"What are people saying about the woman who had that car accident? Didn't it happen here?" A woman in a close-fitting hat and paisley blouse was pointing out the window.

"We're coming up on the spot." Bess slowed the bus. "See that tree where the bark is stripped along the side? That's where she hit it."

All the bus riders chimed in. "She had to be going more than 15 miles an hour for that to happen."

"She claims she swerved to avoid hitting a deer, but I don't believe it."

"I heard she was speeding and plowed through a bench first, which slowed her down. She would have been really hurt if that hadn't happened."

"She'll be out of the hospital in no time and back on the road again. No one wants to give up their license at Regal Crest, no matter what kind of a menace to others they are. They feel it's okay as long as they don't go outside the gate."

"You can't imagine what I see being on the road all day," Bess added. "Cars zipping through stop signs, going the wrong way, ignoring pedestrians in crosswalks. You take your life in your hands when you try to cross the street in Regal Crest. You have to look one way, then the other, and then run!" The bus riders erupted in laughter.

"I have neuropathy. I have no feeling left in my feet," a gray-haired woman turned the conversation to a more serious note. "I can't feel the gas pedal or brake when I drive," she confessed. "But I still take the car out on occasion when the bus has stopped running, and I feel I really have to."

There was a lull in the conversation as people digested what was just said. Bess pulled up to the corner of Elk Court. A West Indian woman who looked to be in her forties was waiting for the bus. She was carrying a big, rectangular, festive green-and-yellow shopping bag almost as wide and as big as herself.

"How are you, Marge? Is everything OK? How is Mrs. Stein?"

Marge swung her bag over the top step and then entered the bus. She looked around. "Hi, Sunny. Hi, Gail." She smiled at the other passengers before turning to Bess. "Mrs. Stein is fine, thanks for asking. I was even able to convince her to go outside and sit on a bench by the fountain yesterday. The weather was so nice. They moved some of the benches from the front of the building though, even the ones with the dedication plaques. Seems the real estate agents didn't want to have too many old and infirm people sitting in the entryways. They thought it was bad for business, or that it would put off the younger people moving in. I wouldn't mind though seeing happy older people enjoying their time in the sun. I'd just think 'look, that could be me one day, happy and relaxed.'"

"Yes, that's a picture," Bess replied.

"But now I'm sad," Marge continued. "I just lost my sister. She died of cancer. She didn't smoke or anything."

"Oh, Marge." Bess glanced over her shoulder. "I am so sorry to hear that, but anyone can die of cancer. It doesn't matter if you smoke or not."

"Secondhand smoke. Our mom and dad smoked. Everyone smoked. They didn't know what she had. She kept going to the doctors for 14 months. By then, it was too late: stage-four cancer. She was only 57 years old."

A gasp went up in the bus. "That's young!" Sunny said.

Marge continued, "She wanted to be cremated."

"Me, too." Bess was very firm in her statement.

"Why?"

"I don't know why. I just do. Burn me up and throw my ashes in the ocean."

"I want to be buried so my children will visit me," Gail chimed in.

"Why would they visit me then? They don't visit me now," the passenger with neuropathy added.

"They can come to the spot where they threw the ashes and visit me then," Bess said.

"They'll just row on by." Everyone turned around to the back of the bus, laughing, to see who made this comment.

"I have a friend whose mother died nine years ago," Marge continued. "Since I've known him, he goes by the cemetery every year on her birthday and leaves a beautiful bouquet of flowers."

"Give me my flowers now," someone quipped.

"No one in our family is cremated," Marge mused. "But I know someone who keeps his wife's ashes in the middle of the dining table. He says hello in the morning. He tells her what he is eating for breakfast. The box is beautiful, but…"

"I think that's sweet," Bess cut in.

"My sister-in-law too. She keeps her husband's ashes in a metal vase in the living room," another passenger added.

"I think that's awful." The tone of Marge's voice was showing frustration. "I want to be buried. I want an open casket from the moment my body is prepared until after the funeral. I want everyone to say 'you look so beautiful.'"

"And do they say that to you now?" one rider said under her breath.

Marge's voice softened. "I went to the market and picked out the most beautiful expensive antique lace as a shroud. I told the Indian salesman I have to be able to fit in it in 10 years or more. He said, 'Are you trying to lose weight?' I said, 'No, it's a shroud.' He was shocked. He said I was too young to be thinking about a shroud."

"You are!" a very elderly lady spoke up for the group. "We're not thinking about it, and we're much older than you."

The bus pulled up on Sunny's block. "Will I see you tomorrow, Sunny? Are you going to the gym?" Bess reached over for the metal handle and swung the door open.

"Yes, I'll try. But if the weather is nice, I'll walk. Get some extra exercise in."

"I admire your discipline. I could use a workout program, too. I do miss seeing you every day on the bus, though."

Sunny waved to the bus as it pulled off, used a plastic hang tag to open the front door, got her mail, took the elevator to the third floor, and entered her apartment. She dropped the mail and her purse on the hallway table and headed to the kitchen. Suddenly, she felt very hungry.

Entering her kitchen always made Sunny smile, and today was no exception. The yellow-and-blue décor was so cheerful, especially when the sun streamed through the wide glass windows in the late afternoon sun. Often, she positioned one of her chairs so that it would be sitting smack in the middle of a ray of sun, and the heat would bake her skin even in the winter months.

Sunny liked the irony of being her age and yet having a retro-style kitchen. In fact, General Electric's latest appliances, in the style of the 1950s, complete with the original GE emblems, were being pitched to millennials. What goes around comes around; what's old is new. She was just sorry she hadn't originally replaced all the appliances as Joe had wanted her to. It seemed so wasteful at the time, given that the ones they had were in perfect working order. True to form, along with Joe's passing, the dishwasher died. Now she had all-new appliances, but Joe wasn't here to enjoy them.

Sunny thought of her friend Barbara's end-of-life philosophy. Now in her 70s, Barbara frames every purchase with her non-future in mind: "This will be my last bed as it has a 20-year warranty; this will be my last car..." Sunny wondered if this was the way people felt when they reached their eighties and nineties. Do they spend each day wondering if this will be their last? Recently, she read a newspaper article about the oldest WWII vet, a 107-year-old man, who had been invited to a state dinner with President Obama. Had he been thinking daily about his impending demise for 27 years? Now that she was living at Regal Crest, many of Sunny's friends were older than she: some were at the age her parents would have been. She'd have to get their opinion on this.

* * *

A wave of tiredness came over Sunny. She looked at the kitchen clock and sighed. It was nowhere near a respectable time to go to bed. Joe used to keep her honest and insist she stay up when she felt this way. He would laugh when she appeared in the living room to kiss him goodnight in her pajamas and night cream at 6 PM, then suggest a list of activities she could do instead. Well, there was no one to stop her now.

Sunny reached into the refrigerator and pulled out a cardboard box containing half a sweet potato pie. At the Regal Crest Book Club meeting a few days ago, it was her turn to buy a thematic snack for the group. The book was about a high school in the 1940s. The food reference she found was about wealthy students being able to afford the ten cents it cost to order pie and cold milk with their school lunch. Hence, the leftover sweet potato pie and bottle of whole milk in her refrigerator.

She started to cut herself a huge chunk of pie, but then decided to just slide the whole remaining pie onto her plate instead. She got a fork and a napkin, and carried everything to the kitchen table.

Sunny lifted the fork and speared a piece of the crust and filling. But as she was bringing it to her mouth, the quiet moment brought the events of the day to the forefront of her mind, and the resulting overwhelming feelings were making her feel sick to her stomach… again. Sunny gagged, pushed the plate away, put her head on the table, and cried.

Chapter 21

# Phil

REPRESENTATIVE PHIL RICHARDS turned from high-fiving the person beside him and scanned the room. Stan was in the far corner, grinning at him. Stan caught Phil's eye, balled his fists, and put both hands in a thumbs-up position. "Yes!" he mouthed.

Sometimes, it felt kind of creepy to have Stan right there, like a faithful dog, glued to his side all the time, anticipating his every move and being, quite frankly, overly solicitous. But Phil felt lucky to have him. Phil was ambitious and needed a way to keep his nose to the ground. Stan, like a frisky puppy, sniffed things out and did the job well. In fact, that's how Phil found out about this meeting. And being here was worth its weight in gold.

The $50,000 a year he was paying Stan in salary was money well spent. He knew that would be a "can't-say-no" amount of money to Stan, given the pennies he was pulling in as a dishwasher at a local Italian restaurant, and that Stan would be forever grateful. And it also ensured his discretion. Sometimes you had to buy things like loyalty. Any good politician knew that.

The one-year anniversary of Stan being an employee was coming up, and Phil would have to figure out a way to continue paying him. This first $50,000 came from the $60,000 he had inherited from his mother when she died suddenly last year.

He thought he was one unlucky son when her kidney cancer was discovered—the unforgiving cancer, they called it. She died at 63, within three months of diagnosis. It was hard losing a parent, even though he was an adult, and even though they were never as close as he wanted them to be. But then he realized he had been spared a bullet. His colleague Ron was always missing roll-call votes because of some emergency that came up with his 91-year-old dad. Ron was always complaining, lamenting about not having a life. Phil was lucky he wouldn't have to go through that. The inheritance was a surprise bonus.

He was sure his mother wouldn't have been happy with how he was buying political favors with her money. But she probably would have been even less happy with how he spent the remaining $10,000 on discreet high-class prostitutes. Well, given his work, he didn't have time to meet anyone, and discretion came at a cost. He didn't want to be, to say quite crassly, caught with his pants down as so many politicians did.

His brother, Alex, was even worse in his choice of how to spend his share of the inheritance. Right after their mother died, the weakness he had been experiencing on his right side had been diagnosed as MS. Although it was a correct diagnosis, the doctor giving the bad news was a charlatan with a promise of a cure. The doctor set him up with a twice-a-week routine of medical steam baths, intravenous medications, megavitamins, and a complex detoxification program. $60,000 was quickly lost down a black hole of treatment. Three months later, all the money was gone, and Alex was left feeling worse than ever.

$120,000. That money represented years of their mother's hard work, scrimping and saving. When put into perspective, that was a lot of money gone down the drain. Sorry, mom!

Phil was in the news and on talk shows quite often, but he wasn't surprised that no one recognized him at this meeting. He went out of his way to keep himself below the radar and nondescript. He made sure to wear striking glasses when he appeared in public, creating a focal point that left out his facial features. He would never be caught wearing one of those ill-fitting toupees that almost every politician seemed to be sporting, even the ones his age and younger. Who wears something like that in real life? And he was lucky to have that 'boy next door, could be anyone' look.

Today, he was dressed simply in dark slacks and a button-down collared white shirt. He had a red tie folded in his back pocket, and a flag pin in his front pocket, ready for his afternoon meeting with some disgruntled constituents.

Phil sat back down, waiting for the room to clear out. The presentation was an interesting concept, for sure. But it was nothing new. Using political clout, laws and regulations to address a social issue had been done before. "Demographic engineering," the experts called it: managing and controlling the population for a wider social good.

Just yesterday in the paper, the sidebar headline was about China changing their one-child policy, successfully put in place in the 1980s to rein in runaway population growth, to now allow couples to have two children. You would think that the government getting in the middle of people's sexual and family decisions by dictating if they can have children and how many would get people's backs up, but they get used to it. It becomes the norm. They find a way to adjust and make it their own, and are willing to step over the line to do that. Sex-selective abortions and infanticides become part of their lexicon. And the same thing would happen with this program. You can bet on it.

Yes, this was something he could sink his teeth into. Phil had been looking for a way to make his mark. And this was it!

# Chapter 22

# Nick

There was a moment of deadening silence. Nick began the process of organizing and stacking his notes, and walked to the side of the podium to signal that the meeting was over. For a moment, people sat still, seemingly dazed by the import of the meeting they had just sat through. Were they understanding it correctly?

For the first time, they avoided eye contact with each other. Connecting, even on this superficial level, would make everything too real. Finally, a few people stretched and turned, scraped back their chairs, stood up, and began putting on their jackets and organizing their things. There was movement in the room again, although with less animation than previously. There was a more somber feeling all around as people headed toward the exit.

One man came up to Nick to shake his hand. "I just want you to know I am with you 100%. We all are. It takes bold action to address a problem such as this."

"I look forward to seeing what we all come up with," another said.

By now, there was a small gathering around Nick. One man reached around the small crowd to pat Nick on the back, and then pulled his hand back to his side and started the quick walk toward the exit. The men waited patiently while the people in line ahead of them said a few words to Nick.

Nick nodded and listened, a smile plastered on his face, and breathed a sigh of relief as the last person in this subgroup asked the last of a series of questions.

*Stupid questions. Really!* Nick thought. *What a bunch of losers.* But he pushed the thought quickly out of his mind. He needed them to get the job done.

Now there were just two people in the room: Mike and a skinny nondescript person, stark in black slacks and a crisp white shirt, who looked vaguely familiar. He kept looking around, waiting for Mike to leave.

Mike was miffed. *Who is this guy? I know I've seen him before.*

The man carried himself as if he were someone important. He rolled back on his heels, settling into a waiting stance.

*Who does he think he is?* Mike's mind was spinning. *Doesn't he realize that I'm important too—that I'm the second half of the team? I carried the first half of the meeting, for God's sake, and would have brought it home myself if Nick hadn't shown up.*

The minutes ticked by and the moment got awkward. Mike finally took the hint and went to the back of the room, so it would appear he was out of earshot.

As soon as Mike stepped back, Phil walked up to Nick and took both of his hands in his. He had a firm, confident grip. "You are just what we need. You are a breath of fresh air."

*Who's 'we'? Need for what?* Nick thought, but waited to hear more.

"It's a solution so simple, yet so complex," Phil continued. "But one I'm willing to take on."

Phil saw the question mark on Nick's face. He took off his glasses and looked straight at Nick.

"You don't know who I am, do you? I'm Phil. Phil Richards. Representative Richards."

Nick took in a large, inaudible breath and reconfigured his face. Representative Richards. His insides leapt. He had seen him once or twice on Fox News, although he looked very different in person. This was quite a coup, but it would be the worst thing to let Phil know that he felt that way and was in awe of this turn of events.

It's a good thing Nick had learned a few tricks about masking emotions from his elder sister Lynn. Lynn had been diagnosed with early-onset Parkinson's disease, like Michael J. Fox. She was lucky not to have the tremors and stiffness so evident in Michael but, to her, the presenting symptom she had was even worse: hypomimia. Lynn would be in a social gathering smiling, but no one would know. Her facial features were stiff and unmoving. When she was sad, you wouldn't know it until tears rolled down her cheeks. Lynn was very embarrassed and eventually stopped socializing and being around people, in effect becoming a hermit.

*Come to think of it...* Nick's thoughts slipped to a side tangent. *We might want to expand our mission to include people like Lynn. What kind of a life do persons with certain disabilities have, anyway? Even though they are young, there is no hope for them to be normal. And talk about draining resources! A boatload of money will be spent on doctor's visits, drugs, tests and treatments over what could be a very long frustrating and unproductive life.* He'd remember to bring this up at the next meeting.

Nick was fascinated by his sister's ailment and how it presented itself. He studied her face and carriage, looking for ways he could incorporate this in his own persona. Lynn would get so mad because he was just staring at her all the time. But he couldn't tell she was mad even then, which excited him about this special skill she had even more.

He practiced in the mirror, thinking about a sad event in his life, such as the day his cat Chuck walked out the fifth-floor window and was found later splattered on the sidewalk below. Then he would check his face, looking in the mirror to see what he had to do to make sure his feelings didn't show.

He would continue his practice, thinking of a happy, gleeful moment that's harder to come by, such as the thrill of hearing the ice cream truck bells ring as a child, and running down from his apartment to the street below. The times he didn't miss it, that is. The thought of the sensation of the cold chocolate coating on his warm tongue made his body shiver. A soft flush spread across his skin. What pleasurable memories. Then he would watch in the mirror to make sure that even though there wasn't a turned-up mouth, there was no twinkle in his eye to give him away.

Nick brought himself back to the present, keeping his face blank. He glanced over to where Mike was standing to see if he was registering anything, but Mike had positioned himself so that it appeared he was engaged in looking over some posters attached to the back wall.

"Nice to meet you, Phil." Nick deliberately didn't use Phil's title. There was no sense in letting him think he was unduly impressed.

But Nick's inner voice was already way ahead of him. With Representative Phil on their team, many more doors would be open. He was sure of it!

What was it that he had heard Phil say just the other day? There was a segment on NBC's *Today* show about the latest news sensation, "The Knockout Game": teenagers punching strangers in the head, unprovoked. They don't say anything or try to rob their victims, which makes it particularly strange. Representative Phil, a solid member of the NRA and proponent of individual gun rights, admitted in his interview that "Packing wouldn't help. You would be blacked out before you could reach for your gun." Nick remembered the segment clearly. Phil faced the television camera head on, and continued. "The best solution is the continued support of the stop-and-frisk policy to keep these losers off the street. Thank God we have a mayor who understands and supports this."

Nick corralled his thoughts and tried to focus on what Phil was saying.

"I understand what you are saying. I know what the real agenda is." Phil paused for emphasis, and to make sure Nick was listening. "But before I put my weight behind your project, I have a task for you: a kind of test."

Nick bristled. Who was Phil to be testing him? All this was his idea, after all.

Phil continued, seemingly totally unaware of how upset Nick was becoming.

"Remember when you were a boy and with your best friend, you pricked your fingers to become blood brothers? Or when you joined a gang or fraternity and had to do something difficult to prove your loyalty? Well, this serves the same purpose. I have to make sure you are totally on board, 100%. So, I'm asking you to identify one person as a candidate for what I'll call 'gentle elimination'. Think about someone close to you. Think about yourself doing them a favor. Take your time. See how it feels. Play around with it in your head. And as you do the deed, think about a way to keep it all low-key. There may be some creative ideas we can adopt."

Phil glanced over in Mike's direction. "I don't want to talk about this in more detail here." Mike was clearly uncomfortable waiting, shuffling his feet and moving his body back and forth. "But let's set a time and place. Suffice it to say that you will be thrilled to have me on board. I can take this to another place. I have the political system well in grasp."

Phil pulled out his iPhone and punched up the calendar app. "I prefer to do it sooner rather than later, so we'll have the whole month before your next meeting to plan and move things along. And do you have notes on what you said today or something in writing? If so, email it to me." Phil opened up his wallet and pulled out a business card, which he handed to Nick. "I'll take this sign-up sheet and make a copy for me, and give it back to you when we meet." Phil took the paper off the front table, folded it up, and put it in his jacket's inside pocket. *"You* have balls. I know a mover and shaker when I see one, and that's the kind of person I want to partner up with.

"My splinter group in the House was trying to figure out a way to solve these health problems: Obamacare, the budget, runaway Medicare, and people not understanding or caring. My neighbor called me up, distressed. She got billed $20,000 for a five-week experimental physical therapy program her doctor put her in to help with her balance. She was distraught. How could it cost so much? But when she realized it would be covered by Medicare, that the taxpayers would in effect be paying for her treatment instead of it coming out her own pocket, she said, 'Oh, well.' People just let things take their own course. Ironically, with our plan, they'll be taking control again. Their fate will be in their own hands. But enough of that. There's time to talk about this later. Let's schedule a date."

Nick's anger was tempered as the compliments rolled off of Representative Phil's tongue. Phil got it: hook, line and sinker. He wouldn't even mind sharing his expanded notes with him. He'd see.

On cue, he reached for his smart phone. He would definitely meet with Phil, if only to see what he had in mind. And in the meantime, he'd have to do some research. Mae always had the TV going on in the background, but on MSNBC, not Fox News. Yes, he knew a little bit about Representative Phil, but he'd have to brush up on him and delve a bit. Thank God for computers and Google. He'd see if it made sense to make the Nick-Mike combo a trio instead of a duo.

Chapter 23

# Mike

Mike appeared not to be listening, but he was straining to hear what the skinny bold man was saying to Nick. "Representative Phil." No wonder he looked so familiar. He took a few steps closer into the room and could hear much clearer now. Phil was slathering Nick with compliments.

Mike was seething. He could feel his blood begin to boil. *What about me?* Despite his mixed feelings about everything, those words crossed his mind before he could stop them. Now Nick and Phil were both reaching for their smart phones. It appeared they were going to set up a follow-up meeting.

Mike waited for Nick to wave him forward and check if the date and time were okay with him, but it never happened. Instead, Phil and Nick locked eyes, shook hands and Phil started walking toward the back of the room, right up the aisle where Mike was standing.

Phil came so close to Mike that for a minute, Mike thought he was going to acknowledge him, perhaps by throwing off a phrase such as, "Good work on the first part of the meeting. I look forward to working with you, too." But that didn't happen. Instead, Phil gave Mike a quick nod before pushing through the back door.

Mike was aware of a familiar feeling coursing through his body. In spite of his buffed-up appearance, he was once again the nerdy kid people ignored and didn't pay any attention to. He felt dissed!

It took a few seconds for the door to settle in place. Mike looked through the small door window and could see Phil's straight back as he walked down the hallway toward a man waiting for him, who was smiling broadly and had a carriage that said, 'I worship you; you are the best thing since sliced bread.'

Mike felt a yearning and emptiness. No one had ever felt that way about him.

Phil put up his hand to give this other man a high-five, and they linked and squeezed each other's fingers before letting go. Phil then let his arm dangle over this man's shoulder in a manly way and steered him around the exit corner.

Mike unconsciously sighed as he turned around and headed to the front of the room. The contrast between the deep connection between Phil and his friend and him and Nick irked Mike.

Nick looked at him and smiled. "Well, what do you think?"

Mike tried to come up with a quick answer, but it was only then that he realized how angry he was, and it was hard to get the words out of his mouth in the way it would be best to say it.

It was only when Nick went on that Mike realized Nick really didn't expect an answer in either case. "I think it went great! At least, as good as I could have expected it to go. Thanks for holding down the fort until I got here."

"It was more than holding down the fort," Mike blurted out. "Am I hearing you correctly? Are you talking about taking people out?"

"Phil got it. He calls it 'gentle elimination.'"

"Who? That guy?" Mike bristled.

"Yes, Phil. Phil Richards, the politician."

Nick looked up at Mike, a disappointed look on his face layered over a smirk. "Don't be so naïve. I'm sure you didn't think the solution would be simple or easy."

"No, but killing people? Because that's what it is. Murdering innocent people."

"Innocent? How innocent? Spending as if there is no tomorrow? Well, I guess there isn't a tomorrow for them," Nick snickered.

"Going to see a podiatrist, a heart specialist, a neurologist, a physical therapist, an ophthalmologist, a dermatologist, and that's for one person in one month. And the treatment, more often than not, is to put on a bandage or two and then start the process all over again when, because of age, things inevitably fall apart a few months down the pike. We all pay for that!

"And for the seniors who don't have health issues, they spend $4,000 on a river cruise, $8,000 on a trip to India, $20,000 for a timeshare, $90,000 for an RV. They are lucky to have been born into a generation that has a stable pension and secure Social Security. By spending, spending, spending, they are thumbing their noses at their children, who are living paycheck to paycheck, and at our generation in general."

Mike's head was spinning. He could feel himself being lured into the arena that had attracted him to Nick and his philosophies in the first place, but he quickly snapped back. "There must be a better way, a way that's not so extreme and desperate." His tone was sounding whiny.

"Sometimes, you have to cut off the festering sore to save a leg. Sometimes, you have to do something in a broad stroke to make an impact. Believe me, if I thought it could be done in another way, I would have suggested it."

"I don't know…" The words were barely out of Mike's mouth when Nick interrupted him.

"Trust me on this. I've been thinking about this much longer than you." Nick turned his back to Mike and started gathering his belongings.

*No, you don't,* Mike thought. *You don't just dismiss me that way.* The familiar feelings were simmering up again. Mike walked two steps toward Nick and reached up to grab his shoulder. Just as Mike was about to make contact, Nick turned around. They were uncomfortably face-to-face, only a few inches apart.

If Nick noticed anything unusual about Mike's stance, he didn't let on. He unobtrusively took a step backward as he talked. "Well, Phil's on board. What a coup. Now that's someone who can move things along."

*As opposed to me?* Mike thought.

Nick continued matter-of-factly. "In fact, he gave us a small job to do: Complete a 'gentle elimination' of someone we know as a test case." Nick's words were calm and measured.

Mike's mind went spinning out of control as he weighed the horrors of this with the deep loss he would feel if cut out of something so cutting-edge and exhilarating.

"I hope I'll be involved in the planning with him." Mike didn't want to sound like he was begging.

"Sure. Sure."

Mike could tell that Nick was already on to the next thing. Well, maybe he'd be on to the next thing, too. All of this was more than he had bargained for and bringing up heavy emotions to boot. He'd have to figure out what to do about it. But in the meantime, he would let Nick think everything was okay. That would be easy to do. He was used to living a lie. His whole persona was a lie, and smarty-pants Nick and his precious pal Phil weren't able to see through that. Ha!

"That's okay with me, Nick." Mike relaxed his stance. "What a team."

# Chapter 24

# Nick

Nick tiptoed into the apartment. He put his backpack on the kitchen table and went looking for Mae. It was only mid-afternoon, but she was lying in bed bundled up in her pajamas, fast asleep. The sheets and blankets were twisted and turned. She must have been flailing again in her sleep.

Just at that moment, Mae moaned and attempted to turn over. Nick waited for her to settle down, then he smoothed the coverings over her. He brushed his hand over her forehead and leaned down to give her a kiss.

"The kiss of death!" Words often went through Nick's head like the credits at the end of a movie. He jerked himself back up and just stood staring at Mae. Of course, she would be his test case. She would be the person he would kill to fulfill Representative Phil's assignment. He would be doing her a favor: an act of kindness.

Nick pulled the cover up further. He remembered when Mae first made this blanket: blue and purple zigzags were crocheted in a large pattern. She went on to do blankets for all her grandchildren. "What are your favorite colors?" she'd ask, and you'd know a blanket was forthcoming. She called it the Crafts Stage of her life when Grandpops first retired. She worked on her crochet and Grandpops would sit by her with his own project, hooking rugs.

The satin trim was now over her mouth and nose, just under her eyes. No, that was too easy, and probably not effective. What about the pillow? Mae's gray hair was splayed over the pillow where her head rested heavy, sunk in the middle. But there was a second pillow on the other side of the bed, probably a habitual remnant from when she shared a bed with Grandpops. The pillowcase was crisp and clean.

Nick picked up the pillow, aware of its softness and its pliability. He held it with two hands, one on each side of the pillow, and began lowering it.

All of a sudden, Mae's eyes snapped opened—sharp, clear, gray eyes staring at the object above her.

"Cloud," she affirmed. "Rain soon." She rolled over to her side, taking the sheets and blankets with her. She was still asleep. Nick could hear her heavy breathing and light snoring.

Frustrated, Nick threw the pillow across the room. His stomach knotted up. He needed to think this through. But first, a tall glass of ginger ale would be just what the doctor ordered.

Five minutes later, he was slouched down at the kitchen table, deep in thought, his long legs flung out in both directions. He swirled the soda in his glass, hearing the ice cubes clink and feeling the cold sweat dripping down the glass and tingling against his fingers.

The deed would have to be done in such a way that no one would suspect anything. It would have to seem like a natural occurrence. That shouldn't be too hard with Mae; she was so far gone. Any minor mishap would be plausible.

As it was, he was always on pins and needles, wondering about the dangers Mae could get herself into. The possibilities were endless. He would just have to pick one and orchestrate it. Perhaps it was lucky after all not to have a caretaker who would get in the way. He had a lot of breathing room. But it was nice having Sunny to watch Mae this morning, so he could focus on his meeting with a clear head.

He wondered how Mike was feeling. Was he feeling this way too? Was he having trouble taking the first step, even though he believed in the importance of the outcome? Or was he, Nick, just a wuss? First, the movie theater fiasco, and now this. With an open fist, Nick slapped the side of his thigh so hard, his fingers stung.

Nick heard a door bang and feet padding in his direction. He looked up to see Mae standing in the doorway. Gold and silver necklaces hung around her neck. Rows and rows of enamel and beaded bracelets circled her arms. There was a jeweled ring on every finger.

"Look what I found." Mae's eyes danced with excitement.

Nick gave Mae an exasperated look. "That's your own jewelry, grandma, every piece of jewelry you own. Let me help you take them off."

Mae took a step back in anger just as Nick reached out for a necklace. His thumb and forefinger were pulling the necklace toward him, and he could feel the pressure against the back of Mae's neck. He pulled harder, and found himself trying to twist it tight across the front.

"Ouch! You're hurting me!" Nick was sure that Mae's screams were loud enough to be heard in the hallway. He'd have to be careful. He dropped the necklace and watched it snap against Mae's chest. Mae was looking around, her face blank.

Nick let a few seconds pass. "You must be hungry after that long nap. Let me fix you something to eat." He pulled out a slice of white bread and slathered it with peanut butter.

"Thanks, Daddy." Mae smiled and held the bread up to her face, licking the peanut butter off with her tongue.

*Perhaps next time, I could sprinkle the bread with something poisonous,* Nick thought. *I'll have to look it up. But that may be too obvious and easy to trace back to me.*

What about Mae making toast and trying to take it out with a metal fork? What about cooking in the microwave with an aluminum pan? Can those things really take you out?

Nick's head was pounding. There was some Excedrin in the guest bathroom. Mae was still engaged with her bread, now peanut butter-less and soggy. It would only take a minute.

He left the room, thinking about the danger of having the medicine cabinet unlocked. People didn't think of it with elders, but to be vigilant, you needed an open-proof latch, just like you'd have for a toddler. Otherwise, Mae could accidentally swallow a whole bottle of meds.

That's one more way to off Mae. Nick filed this option in the back of his head with the others.

When Nick went into the kitchen again, the refrigerator was ajar, the jelly jar was out and open, and there was jam all over the counter, over Mae's face and pajamas, and stuck in the jewelry.

Mae was in the middle of it all, grinning. "Jelly. Peanut butter and jelly."

Nick sighed. "Let's take a bath." This was one job that Nick hated. He took Mae's hand and led her to the bathroom.

It took a long time to remove all the jewelry. Nick filled the sink with hot water. In went the sticky necklaces, bracelets and rings. He added a couple of squirts of Ivory liquid to the mix.

He turned around. Mae had taken off her pajamas, but had forgotten she was taking a bath, or that she was naked for that matter. She was looking in the mirror, making faces at herself.

"Look. Funny lady."

Nick knew this was his grandmother, but he couldn't help but think of her as a woman. He glanced over her body. Her skin was dry and folded with crusted patches. Her breasts hung flat against her chest, the nipples narrowed and wrinkled. Her pubic hair was silver-white, thin, growing haphazardly and clearly hadn't been shaped in years.

Nick thought about Cheryl. She was so proud of her firm body. Her skin was soft, supple and glowy. Nick loved touching it. Her bush was thick and curly, and was pointed in a perfect V. Nick loved putting his hand down there, feeling the hairs between his fingers and listening to her purr.

He had seen pictures of Mae when she was younger, looking out at him, sepia-toned in a gold gilded frame, with a carriage that had the same body confidence as Cheryl's. And with age comes all this. Nick felt sad.

Mae was still at the mirror, now preening and fluffing her hair. She had been so proud of her full mane and how she was able to wash and style it herself. She picked the hair dryer off the counter, pushed on the switch, and felt the hot air swirling against her face.

The cord was long, and Mae held on tightly to the handle as she tried to enter the tub. Nick caught her by the elbow to steer her in, then noticed the instrument and pried it from her grip. Another close call. Mae electrocuted with her hair dryer: clearly a believable scenario. Being well-groomed was important to the ladies at Regal Crest. He saw them across campus, with their hair freshly teased and sprayed and their fingernails newly painted baby pink.

Nick sat with the hairdryer in his lap, and then turned it on low. Mae was sitting with her back against the bath pillow, slapping the water so that it splashed in the air. Nick moved the dryer closer, inch by inch, to the waves Mae was creating. The nozzle was seconds away from making contact, and Nick found himself quickly jerking his hand back. A pain seared through his body. He was hopeless!

Mae almost fell as she left the bathtub, and Nick caught her without thinking. Another opportunity passed. Angry with himself, he slapped his thigh again and again until the stinging radiated down his leg.

A half-hour later Mae was back in bed again, in clean pajamas, a half-smile on her face, lightly dozing. Nick sat in a stiff upright chair by her side, his head in his hands, his body shaking. Suddenly, he jumped up, grabbed his jacket, cell phone and keys; and rushed to the front door. Right now, he could use something stronger than the soft drinks Mae kept in her refrigerator.

As Nick bolted out the door, an elderly gentleman, balancing on two metal arm canes, was shuffling past Mae's apartment. Nick ran right into him, pushing him sharply against the back wall. The man crumpled to the floor in a heap, and looked sideways up at Nick with an astonished look on his face before dropping his head on the carpeting, his neck twisted and mangled. His chest moved up and down quickly. There was a gurgling sound and then stillness.

Nick looked down at the body beneath him, astonished. He poked the form with the tip of his shoe, but there was no movement. He got down on his knees and put his index finger under the man's nose. He wasn't breathing.

Nick leaned back on his heels. Two thoughts came to him at the same time: *It was just a horrible accident*, and *Whoo-hoo! I completed the assignment!*

Nick took out his cell phone and dialed 911.

# Chapter 25

# Phil

After much high-fiving and shoulder-slapping, Phil stepped out of the passenger side of the yellow Jeep, turned around and gave a final wave to his sidekick. He entered the sleek glass-and-steel apartment building and tersely greeted the doorman before slipping into the dimly lit, smoky-colored elevator. Everything about this building was slick and cool, and that's the way Phil liked it.

He put the key into the lock and entered the foyer. The bright afternoon sun was crisp and white and streamed into the room from the wide, expansive floor-to-ceiling windows, giving everything an icy effect.

It was a small living space—there was just one other room to the side, with a double-sized bed jammed into the corner—but it worked for Phil. And he wasn't much different than the other politicians on the hill. True, he was here full-time, and it was his only residence. Most of the others had families in stately residences stashed away in their home states, and kept a small efficiency apartment in DC. But in terms of living styles, while Congress was in session, he blended in with the rest.

He looked around him and sighed. Now it was time for the hard work. Phil unbuttoned the top two buttons on his shirt to release the starched collar from his neck, and walked to the far corner of his living room where he had a meditation area set up. A thick tasseled pillow with a green-and-black tapestry cover was facing a wall covered with pictures of East Asian scenery: golden temples, white mountaintops, and sari-clad peasants. On the center of the wall was a narrow shelf filled with metal and stone deities. This part of his life was one of the reasons he never had visitors. He didn't want to share. It was incongruous. Questions would be asked. They wouldn't understand.

Phil lowered himself onto the pillow and reached over to press the on-button on the iPod right by him. The repeating sound of "ohm" was barely audible in the background. Phil closed his eyes and almost immediately was in a trance. His body was straight and upright, but at the same time relaxed. His breath and the sound of "ohm" became the focal points. His chest moved in and out—deep breaths, but at a slowing pace.

Minutes went by, and then an hour. Phil's eyes snapped open. "I got it!" He reached over for the note pad he kept in this corner and started scribbling away. Fifteen minutes later, he sat back with a satisfied look as he reviewed seven pages of notes.

It was really very simple. The key to the action plan is that Regal Crest was so large, it was almost a political entity of its own: 7,000 people, but in a dense area of only 800 acres, the size of New York's Central Park. They could easily be isolated. And it was in the middle of a lower-class ethnic community consisting of poor people, just struggling to make it and who did not have the time to think about politics. They barely bothered to vote every four years, and the turnout for off-year elections was dismal. Yet they would notice and appreciate an uptick in their cash flow. That would make sure they were firmly on board. A proposition could easily get by them.

Regal Crest had a strong Democratic Party and Republican Party, too. He would have to research to see who the leaders—the movers and shakers—were. But it was all in the packaging. After all there was a reason why so many scams were targeted at older people. He'd just have to figure out a way to make it happen.

Yes, that was it. Start small, then test it out with a strong foundation. Keep it a bit under the radar. It would be easy to expand once it was a normal part of life.

# Chapter 26

# Sunny

SUNNY SAT IN the meeting, half-daydreaming and half-listening. What was it about older people that made them take things so seriously? Did they really miss the power and prestige of their former jobs so much that little things became so important?

The president of the organization, Mildred, had been talking for the last half-hour about the difficulties involved in hiring a bus for a museum trip; and making it much more drawn-out and complicated than it needed to be. Now, having decided to organize a carpool instead, she insisted the trip would only take an hour despite the swell of protests from the audience, whose collective experiences on the highways said otherwise. Control of the meeting was lost as everyone turned to the people at their table to share their stuck-in-traffic stories, or to lean in to the person next to them to complain about Mildred's leadership style.

Just as Mildred was on the brink of bringing things back to order with a few raps of the gavel and some throat-clearing into the microphone, there was a ground swell in the back of the room as five people entered late in tandem, highly unusual for Regal Crest, whose motto is: "At Regal Crest, if you're on time, you're late."

"There was a fire in Building 2." The woman leading the group walked to the front of the room by the podium. She was wearing a gold sequined cap. A matching shawl was flung over a black t-shirt and jeans. Sunny recognized this as an attempt to make the outfit she was wearing fancier, so she'd be appropriately dressed for the meeting. "The police cordoned off the area. We weren't allowed to leave until now."

"I heard someone died," a woman in the audience shouted out.

"She tried to take her life," another added.

"I don't know about all that," the cap lady continued. "I did hear it was a woman with an oxygen tank, on her balcony smoking a cigarette. 92 years old. She had just sent her aide to Mega Supermarket to fill a prescription."

Sunny's ears perked up. Ever since all this stuff with Nick, everything was suspect. Was the plan still just on paper, or were steps being taken to implement it? Looking back at the meeting last week, Sunny chided herself. Even given the difficulty of having Mae in tow, she wished she had stayed until the end. *I probably missed something important*, she surmised. *Miss Marple would have done better.* Despite her dark thoughts, Sunny found herself smiling inwardly at her private joke.

The new arrivals were settling in the room. Although everyone was still chatting, nothing new was being said about the incident. Sunny went back to her thoughts. It seemed like every day there was a new notice of a neighbor's passing slipped in the plastic frame on the long hall table across from the elevator, not unexpected in a community where the minimum age for residency was 55 years old, and so many people were 90 years old and above. It seemed more frequent now than Sunny remembered, but perhaps it was because she had all of this on her mind. Where did natural happenings and Nick's plans begin and end? Sunny feared it was a blurred line.

In this case, why would a person with an oxygen tank smoke cigarettes? Why would a 92-year-old commit suicide? It seemed to Sunny that if you made it that long, you should just as well keep on going. And fire is scary. Why choose to go that way when you can just take a pill?

Sunny's reveries were broken by a pull on her coat sleeve. Her good friend Martha was signaling that the meeting was about to end. The president, having given up all hope of bringing the meeting back to order, was waving her gavel while trying to shout above the din and chatter to remind people of the date and time of the next gathering.

"Let's get out of here. We'll lose our lunch reservations in the Patio Room."

Leaving was a slow process. Everyone was milling around and talking, and Sunny got caught up in the goings-on. Even though she could see Martha by her side, impatiently tapping her foot and checking her watch, it was hard to extricate herself from Alice, who she was chatting with now. Alice was basically lonely. For Alice, this might be the last time she'd have an opportunity to interface with another person until the meeting next week.

Martha finally took Sunny's arm and dragged her out into the Clubhouse hallway. The restaurant was on the other side of the building, and there was already a stream of people headed in that direction. The club bulletin boards, the art display, and the pictures from the photography club were a blur as they rushed to the restaurant. All the tables were full; but Cynthia and Denise were already there, waving to them from a corner booth.

Sunny walked over, gave each of them a hug, and then slid along the banquette to the far wall. It was safe here to just put your purse on the floor. She looked around. As expected, just about everyone had gray hair, many with walkers parked by their side. It was only on Sundays that the demographics changed as children and grandchildren came to visit.

Sunny remembered having lunch with her friend, Ros, now almost thirty years ago, when she was in her forties. For some reason, the restaurant they were in attracted groups of women across the age spectrum. Ros pointed to the table on each side of them. On one side was a group of women in their twenties. They were all wearing colorful business suits with low-cut tanks under tight jackets, their makeup expertly applied, their hair fresh and shiny. There was a lift and excitement in their enunciations. On the other side was a group of women in their sixties or more, not unlike Sunny and her friends now. Ros said, "That was us twenty years ago; that will be us in twenty years." *Ros was right*, Sunny thought now.

For some reason, this concept had a big impact on her and she thought of it now as she looked around. At the next table was a group of women having dessert and winding up their discussion. Sunny eavesdropped as she settled into her seat. One woman was telling an animated story about a wonderful vacation to a sumptuous retreat in Orlando.

"The house was so big. It was like a mansion with a full kitchen, like the ones you see on the Home and Garden Network. We had our own private pool." The woman paused in her telling, leaving an opening for one of the other women to reply. There was a question mark in one friend's voice and a puzzled look on her face.

"But did they play bridge?"

Sunny finished her meal, folded her napkin next to her plate, leaned back in her chair, and looked warmly at the women around her. These women, Martha, Cynthia and Denise, were important in her life. Their monthly luncheons kept her grounded and connected; and she was able to reach out to them for support and comfort for big things, such as when Joe died, but also for the little things, such as problems with a doctor.

How many times in the conversation today did she want to say something about Nick and The Plan, and the scary things she was finding out? If she could, she would casually bring it up in conversation between Denise talking about how hard it was to follow her exercise routine and Cynthia sharing the latest gossip from her Stitching Club.

She'd say, "You'll never believe what I found out. It scares me to death." Or perhaps she'd say, "Something important is happening here, and I need your advice." They would recognize the urgency just from the tone of her voice.

She wished she could unburden herself with what she had found out and was struggling with, but knew she couldn't. It was too much to ask of them. Why give them her albatross to struggle with, or change their rosy perspective on their Regal Crest lives?

A week had passed since Sunny had crashed Nick's meeting, and she could not bring herself to move forward or address the problem. It was just easier to put her head in the sand. Whenever she turned her mind to it, she heard Nick's words reverberating in her head. But then she thought of the Nick she knew, and nothing seemed to fit in place.

Suddenly, she wanted to live. She didn't realize how important life was to her until there was this possibility that it would be gone. As she walked across campus, she saw people differently. She wanted to be older like Mae and the others one day. Once, she went to the gym and she saw a woman working out, carrying her walker from one machine to the next and working with a trainer; she thought, *What's the point?* Then she heard that the woman was 91 years old, and that changed her perspective. Sunny wanted to be that 91-year-old one day. Before, she just thought she would die one day, sooner or later. Now, longevity seemed important and precious.

She knew she would have to start doing something about Nick and The Plan and not be lulled into complacency. But the more days that passed, the less real it became. Now it was like watching a TV sitcom. She was in her living room, a snack on a tray in her lap, her head thrown back, just laughing and laughing.

# Chapter 27

# Nick

Nick's hand slipped as he pulled the razor over his course stubble, which represented seven days of growth. He had never been good at growing beards—he was forever the baby face.

A tiny drop of blood began oozing from a small cut. He went over by the toilet, took off a square of paper from the roll, and stuck it to his face.

Nick had not been feeling good about himself ever since he offed Mr. Barnes a week ago. That was part of the problem. He kept thinking about it as offing him rather than what it really was, an accident. He couldn't get the extinguished look in the old man's eyes out of his head, the shock etched across his face.

*An accident, an accident, an accident.* Nick repeated the mantra in his mind, as he had been doing over and over again since last Tuesday. But there was always a relentless truth in the background he couldn't cover up—the fact that an important byproduct of the accident was that it tied everything together with a little neat bow, at least for now.

The question remained: how would he handle the next step in the rollout? Just thinking about it made him break out in a cold sweat. Nick hung his face over the sink and threw tepid water on it.

He had to pull himself together and get back to a normal life. That's why he finally answered Cheryl's phone calls and texts.

Cheryl was understandably pissed. They had been dating for a few months, and as far as Nick was concerned, she was the ideal girlfriend. Not only was she sexy and beautiful, but she also understood that a lot of his free time had to be used to take care of Mae. She was empathetic when he lost his job. But he hadn't called her in over a week. This "dropping out" and feeling sorry for himself was unacceptable to her.

"You're not the first person who has lost a job or had to take care of an elderly relative," she admonished, then she softened her stance. "Let me help you. Let me in."

"Yeah, right." Nick wished he could tell her, but what would he say? "I have this plan to eliminate old people and pave the way for young people to have the resources they need. There are groups of people who are willing to walk the walk with me. I don't know why I latched onto this idea, but I did. Now it's gotten out of hand. It's scaring me."

No, this was something he'd have to keep to himself.

Cheryl was stopping by, then they would go out. She always liked to leave from his place, rather than have Nick pick her up, so she could say hello to Mae.

*I'm so lucky to have such a thoughtful girlfriend,* Nick thought before his mind switched to the dark side. *Or is she just checking to make sure I'm taking care of Mae okay?*

Nick looked at the marble-and-gold clock on the bathroom sink. She'd be here in only a few minutes. She was very punctual. He hoped Mae hadn't gotten into anything while he was washing up; that would embarrass him.

Five minutes later, Nick was out in the living room, his face clean-shaven, his eyebrows trimmed. He was wearing a white polo shirt and medium-blue pleated jeans. Mae was sitting by the window where he left her, the afternoon sun glistening through her gray hair. Nick went over and stroked her head so she would know he was there. She looked up at him and smiled. Nick recognized that look. She was lost in some memory.

The doorbell rang. Cheryl stepped forward and gave Nick a deep hug and then a nip on the ear, her eyes laughing. He pulled her in tight and could feel the beginning throbs of his body against hers.

She stepped around him and over to the window. "Hi, Miss Mae."

It was clear from the look on Mae's face that she didn't recognize who was greeting her.

"It's Cheryl. Nick's girlfriend."

There was a flicker of recognition that quickly slipped away.

Cheryl took Mae's hand in hers and patted it. "You look great." She looked over at Nick and smiled. "It's a beautiful day, and I haven't seen Nick in forever. We'll probably go for a long walk and end up at the Thai restaurant across town. Should we bring you something back?"

"Don't like Thai food."

"Okay. Why don't we make you a snack before we go? Give us a few minutes."

Cheryl headed toward the kitchen, but was pulled to the side by Nick. He hugged her tight and began nuzzling her neck, his breath hot across her shoulder. Cheryl's body responded. It had been a long time. She lifted her head and gave him a deep kiss. He wrapped his fingers around the yards of fabric in her silver-gray dress, again drawing her closer, and then began to gently push her toward his room.

"I don't think..." Cheryl's voice was muffled as Nick continued to cover her mouth with kisses. She fell limp against him. She had been in Nick's room a few times, so the sparse furnishings didn't surprise her. He led her to the bed, not losing contact as he loosened his belt buckle. "Are you sure...?"

"Yes... Yes," Nick groaned. He pushed his hand against Cheryl's breasts and moved them around in deep circles. Then he pulled down the straps, one at a time, releasing the flesh and rolling each nipple between his thumb and forefingers.

Cheryl caught her breath and sighed. Nick stopped to pull off his shirt. Cheryl pulled up her skirt and put her thumb in the side of her panties. She was wearing an old-style crinoline to give the skirt body, and now it was scratching against Nick's bare chest. She pulled off her thong and tossed it on the floor.

Their momentum quickened. Nick pulled down his pants around his knees and straddled Cheryl. She pulled the skirt of her dress up higher and raised her body to ease his entry. Nick grabbed himself and rubbed around Cheryl's opening, loving her whimpering, watching the pleas and deepening color of her eyes before pushing it inside. He hadn't felt this good and in control in days. The pace quickened further. The tiny twin bed scratched against the floor and knocked against the back wall.

"I'm coming…" Nick's words were muffled by Cheryl's hand over his mouth, although she could barely contain the sounds coming from her own body.

One final thrust would do it. Nick pulled his body up. Cheryl whimpered as their bodies snapped apart. She was very wet, and Nick planned a mega re-entry.

"Do it. Do it." Cheryl's words were quick and shrill. "Please…"

Nick laughed and began to lower his body onto Cheryl's.

Suddenly, they heard the door bang open. Mae was standing in the door frame, her face red, her veins bulging.

"Robbie! What are you doing?" Nick recognized his father's pet name. "Robbie! Bad boy. And who is this slut?" Mae picked up Cheryl's thong and tossed it onto the bed.

"I told your father he should have the talk with you. But noooo, he thought 13 was too young. And here you are! Probably don't even know about condoms. And if you think I'm going to look after your bastard child, girlie, you have another thing coming. Get dressed!" Mae stomped out of Nick's bedroom, slamming the door behind her.

Nick rolled off of Cheryl. There was barely room for them side by side on the twin bed. His body was tense. His penis lay limp between his legs. How did he end up here, in a narrow bed, left hanging, and being scolded by an 80-something-year-old woman? He was a grown man!

Cheryl swung her feet over the side of the bed to sitting position and began straightening her clothes. "We shouldn't have… in her place…"

"Shhh. It's my place too… for now."

"But still…"

Nick sat up and gave Cheryl a light kiss to keep her from talking. For him, the moment for relief had passed him by. Already, all the angst from the past week was flooding back.

A few minutes later, they walked back into the living room. Nick was holding Cheryl's hand to reassure her.

Mae was sitting by the window, the last afternoon glow sinking below the horizon. She turned her head, looked over at Nick and Cheryl, and smiled. "Sandwich?" she asked.

Chapter 28

# Phil

P HIL OPENED THE latch on the flap of his worn leather briefcase, pulled out a folder, emptied the contents on his desk, and flipped through the pages one last time. Stan was always on time, and always made that clear by impatiently leaning on the shrill horn of the yellow Jeep. That meant that he had exactly 18 minutes to double-check, and if needed, triple-check that everything was correct and in place.

Nick had sent his notes and email files to Phil. Interesting! Phil read them over and over: the building blocks for his own ideas. All week, he had left his mind empty, so the ideas could percolate. When he felt his mind could not hold on anymore, he'd spill it out on paper, or if it was the middle of the night or early in the morning, into a tape recorder by the side of his bed. Yes, paper and ink were a little bit old-school, but Phil found he could think best with the weight of a pen in his hand and he wouldn't have to worry about an electronic paper trail. His garbage can was filled with crumpled papers. He'd have to remember to empty it and take the contents to the shredder, and erase the voice recordings, too.

Regal Crest was the perfect place to put this plan into place. It was self-isolated but big enough that it was a political entity, a governing body all by itself, contributing to the broadest participation of senior voters of any state. The few surrounding communities that made up the 26$^{th}$ voting district that Regal Crest was part of were mostly low-income, struggling neighborhoods. The residents were mostly renters focused on subsistence, living from day to day. They didn't have the time and energy to vet candidates or proposals and propositions. They were so disenfranchised, they didn't even bother to come out and vote. Regal Crest's interests were up front and center. As Regal Crest votes, so goes the county.

This fact wasn't lost on politicians. The Republicans, Democrats and Independents alike made many visits to the Regal Crest campus to present their case. The Democratic Club, the Republican Club and the League of Women Voters all had their pick of presenters for their monthly meetings. The Regal Crest News had full-page ads from various candidates.

In fact, the politicking was so much that residents complained. One letter to the editor of the *Regal Crest News* requested that paid political ads be eliminated completely: "Help me understand. Why do political articles appear on pages 2, 7, 13, 18, 21, 32 and 44? This is our paper, a paper for the residents, and should focus on news about Regal Crest."

It was easy to reach out to the residents of Regal Crest. They had their own zip code and phone book. In fact, Phil had gotten complaints over the years from Regal Crest seniors getting unneeded solicitations, many that bordered on scams. There was a certain predator type that knew how to take advantage of old people's weaknesses: their worry about money, wanting to grow the money they have, and getting something for free. Telemarketers would sit with the Regal Crest phone book, cold-calling page after page until they snagged someone in their net.

It was a shame to think it, but the same dynamics could work in his favor.

Regal Crest could be the test case, a trial run, the perfect test location for what Phil was loosely calling in his mind "The Senior and Society Betterment Plan (SSBP)". The key to making it work would be to implement it slowly and put the pieces in place one at a time. It's amazing how easily people get used to things once they've been exposed to it for a while and it has become the norm.

Phil remembered studying in his government classes about the institution of Medicare, for example. People were up in arms at the time. Now, they would fight tooth and nail against any whisper of it being taken away. It would be the same thing with Obamacare. Five years from now, people will have forgotten the dissension over its implementation that is so prevalent now after they took advantage of the pre-existing conditions, widespread coverage and other benefits that are part of the plan; and it became part of the new normal for them. It's like the story of the frog in the pot. If the water is hot and you put the frog in the pot, he will jump out. But if you put him in a pot of cool water and slowly increase the temperature, he will remain in the pot until completely cooked.

Phil was amazed at how this principle worked, even at the simplest level. For example, to encourage environment compliance, a state law was put into place charging a nickel if you asked for a plastic bag when buying groceries. A nickel is a small amount of money. You wouldn't think it could underpin a movement. People grouched at first, but the politicians held their ground. Grocery stores started selling cloth shopping bags for $.99. Clubs and events started handing out reusable bags that were user-friendly, easy to fold and lightweight as come-ons and premiums. Before you knew it, more and more people were bringing their own bags when shopping. When Phil was in Mega Supermarket the other day, sporting a beaked hat and sunglasses, to purchase a pint of Cherry Garcia ice cream and a six-pack of local craft beer, he noticed that just about everyone was using their own bags. In fact, despite his attempt at camouflage, he was the outlier, leaving the supermarket with two plastic bags. If this could work with grocery bags, he had no doubt the principle would work for his project, too.

So how would it work? Phil flipped through the pages once again. His heart thumped in his chest. His idea was brilliant.

The best way to make inroads is through Social Security. That had become a government benefit that people saw as an entitlement. There was a lot of debate on the Hill about making changes to the Social Security laws to make it viable so that it would be there for future generations. According to current calculations, the Social Security Trust would run out in 2034. Every time making changes to the Social Security program was put on the table by politicians, the AARP would shoot it down and seniors would be up in arms. But people were getting used to reductions in Social Security being thrown in the hat whenever there was a question about balancing the budget. So people wouldn't be surprised with the introduction of a bill that tweaked Social Security as a solution to make things work.

According to Phil's plan, all seniors would start collecting Social Security at 65. This would be simpler and cleaner than what's currently in place: starting reduced benefits at 62, and receiving full benefits depending on one's date of birth. Also, at 65, they would receive a bonus: a lump sum of $30,000, tax-free (equivalent to two years of benefits for the average recipient).

Seniors would be given three options for the lump sum:

Option One: Use the Lump Sum for Oneself:

This money allows for funding and completing bucket-list items, such as travel and moving expenses during prime retirement years, and will stimulate the economy. Having this discretionary money on hand will provide an extra incentive for seniors to leave the workforce and free up jobs for young people.

Option Two: Grandchild Infusion:

Seniors could use the lump sum to gift to their grandchildren. To incentivize this option, an extra 50% or $15,000 will be added to the amount gifted, totaling $45,000.

Option Three: Match the Lump Sum with Own Investment Dollars:

A tax credit for the additional $45,000 will be provided for the senior and grandchild.

At age 69½, seniors would receive another payment from the government of $5,000 in the form of a voucher, good for a year, to be used for a 70$^{th}$ birthday celebration. Hall space, food, photo, and clothing vendors who will accept vouchers will be government-certified. A whole industry could blossom from this, and it would be a way to create additional jobs—like the Civilian Conservation Corps (CCC) in the 1930s during the Great Depression. In time, the 70$^{th}$ birthday party would become part of the culture and a rite of passage such as a christening, a bar mitzvah or sweet sixteen celebration.

*Nothing is for free,* Phil thought as he put an asterisk at the bottom of the page describing the program. "*All seniors participating in this program will be enrolled in the E-PEP initiative: The Elderly Partnership and Enhancement Project—a senior betterment program."

There's no need to let people know what the acronym really stands for. Seniors will have a robust, fulfilling, rich retirement, albeit short, without putting society on the brink of bankruptcy.

Phil put it all in chart form. That is, everything except the details of how the "Elderly People Elimination Project" would work. There's no need to have a paper trail about that. Maybe he would outline the steps with Nick in person. He'd have to see how he felt when they met.

But meanwhile, the chart for the overview would work. He found from experience that simplifying things to their basic level made it easy to understand. He had seen many bills and proposals get waylaid because they were hung up in pages and words.

Phil made three copies of the chart: one for him, one for Nick, and an extra one, just in case. His copy was marked up with a purple pen and orange highlighter. He liked to mess with whoever was sitting next to him at the long conference tables cramped into the small meeting rooms on the Hill. He watched them uncomfortably looking over their shoulders when they thought he didn't notice.

*Why all the colors?* they were probably thinking. *Well, wouldn't you like to know?* They were all so shallow. Actually, purple and orange were his school colors from Jefferson High School, an era that contained the sweetest moments of his life. It was at "the Jeff" that he fell in love with politics and public speaking. All the other boys in the debate club were just like him—sharp, topical, glib, and always questioning—

but he was the only one who broke through and turned his passion into a profession.

Although Phil made sure he had the appearance of being casual when he pulled out his cell phone after the meeting last week to set a date with Nick, the time he chose was very calculated. It was exactly a day to the week that Nick had held his meeting a week ago.

Was Nick serious, or just a lot of hot air? It was important for him to know the answer to this before he stuck his neck out too far. A week was enough time for Nick to make some headway on the next steps, but also gave them three weeks remaining to do some serious planning before the follow-up meeting was scheduled.

He had already thrown some tidbits of their idea out there, and the people closest to him were waiting with bated breath. He didn't want to tip his hand too soon. It was very important that this be implemented under the radar and in a thoughtful, calculated way.

Implementation looked difficult on the outside, but it really was very easy. It all came down to understanding the different interest groups, the players—their strengths and weaknesses, and then how they could be manipulated. And Phil prided himself on being the king of manipulation. He was a politician, after all.

Chapter 29

# The Senior and Society Betterment Plan Chart

THE SENIOR AND SOCIETY BETTERMENT PLAN (SSBP)*
Enhancement of Social Security Benefits
to Enrich All Generations**

Description of Proposed Bill

The main purpose of the proposed bill is to strengthen the Social Security Program to make it most effective in the service of seniors, and make sure it's a viable program for future generations.

In addition to its initial purpose of creating continuous income for seniors in retirement, these changes also create potential funding of younger generations and the timely transfer of assets from seniors to them to financially strengthen their position at an earlier stage of their lives.

Streamlining the Social Security Program will make it more efficient and less costly. In addition, it is an economy booster and job creator. Many of the initiatives that will be put in place will require additional labor across a variety of industries.

Providing lump-sum income for seniors and younger people will boost the economy as money will now be readily available for discretionary expenditures.

For seniors, it will enable them to front-load their dream retirement activities such as traveling, taking courses, or moving to a retirement community. Younger people will have the assets needed to get a graduate degree, put a down payment on a house, fund a wedding/honeymoon, or cover their ongoing expenses without going into debt.

## SSBP

| WHAT'S NEW/WHAT CHANGES | WHAT WE GAIN |
| --- | --- |
| Everyone collects full Social Security benefits at 65. Not collecting at 62, but the age of full-benefit eligibility doesn't increase. | Streamlines Social Security — less costly. Get full benefits sooner. |
| Lump-sum payment at 65 of $30,000, equivalent to two years of Social Security for the average person. | Discretionary income at retirement to front-load their bucket lists. Stimulates the economy. |
| "The Grandchild Infusion": 50% bonus ($15,000 additional) if the lump-sum payment is gifted to grandchildren. | Knowledge that next generation is taken care of; can participate in advising how money is spent. Stimulates the economy. |
| Match $45,000 Grandchild Infusion with own assets. If gifted, an additional $45,000 will be provided as a tax incentive, in the form of credit for the senior and grandchild. | Further secure future generations. Stimulates the economy. |
| $5,000 voucher for 70th birthday celebration. | Incentivize society to celebrate/appreciate the elder generation. Support for and job creation in the party and event-planning industries. |

*If passed, this bill will be enacted in the 26th District for the next five years. At the end of this time period, assuming its success, plans will be made to roll it out to the rest of the country.

**All seniors participating in this program will be enrolled in the E-PEP initiative: The Elderly Partnership and Enhancement Project.

# Chapter 30

# Sunny

The clock radio alarm went off, startling Sunny awake. She barely had time to roll over before she heard a second buzzing sound coming from her smart phone. She always set a double alarm when she had something important to do. Now, what was it?

Sunny sat up, her feet dangling over the edge of the bed, and unconsciously straightened her rounded posture. She didn't need a mirror to know she had smut in the corners of her eyes and dry spittle from the side of her mouth across her cheek: another downside of growing old. It was better she didn't have someone to share her bed and to see her at her worst each morning, although Joe insisted he didn't care. He used to say that he loved all aspects of her: the silky smooth; the rough and tumble; the good and bad.

Even after all this time, it was hard to get used to being alone. Just the other day, one of her best friends lost her husband, and Sunny could feel her pain as if it were her own.

There was an article in a recent issue of the *Regal Crest News* discussing this very topic, called "The Benefits of a 50-Year Marriage". It talked about the little things that are missed when a spouse dies—commiserating over the headlines of the day's newspaper; the conviviality of eating together, but saying nothing for the entire meal because there's no need to; supporting each other during treatments and doctor's visits.

If Joe were here, they'd be having small talk about silly, insignificant things. She used to get mad when he asked stupid questions over and over, or fretted over whether it was worth an extra 15 cents to buy gourmet coffee when there was so much important stuff going on in the world. But Joe would just shrug and say, "You have to live the micro with the macro." And when she worried over not having time to do everything she had planned in a day, he would say, "What is it I always say? The only thing you have to do is pay taxes and die." She missed his witticisms.

They would watch each other serendipitously when they seemed to be having age-related problems. When Joe put his shoe on the pantry shelf instead of in the boot tray, she got concerned. And whenever she couldn't remember something, Joe would say "Uh-Oh" and they would both laugh it off. It was all in fun. Neither one of them really thought that anything serious was happening. Now, she had no one to help put it all in perspective. Were her brief lapses of memory just a normal part of aging? Or could it be the beginning of dementia, or worse?

Mostly, Sunny found herself wondering what Joe's take would be on the various things happening in her life. What would he say about Nick and his meeting, for example? Would he take it seriously, or just laugh it off and think she was making a mountain out of a molehill?

That was it! She had gone to bed with the resolve to do something about the Nick situation. What had she decided? She remembered feeling satisfied with whatever her decision was, and falling comfortably into a deep sleep. How frustrating this is!

Precious time was passing. She had to, at the very least, find out more of what was happening with Nick and his plan. It was tempting to just ignore it, but there was too much at stake. Sunny waffled between thinking about what she could really do and thinking about how her role model, Miss Marple, would take the problem firmly in hand.

And what specifically would Miss Marple do? As Sunny posed the question to herself, her idea from the night before came to the forefront of her mind. Eureka! She remembered now. She had decided to find a way to forge a deeper relationship with Nick so he would trust her, and quite frankly, so she could snoop. She had been looking for someone who could assist her with her rental properties—a cross between a handyman, a rent collector, and a guy Friday.

If Nick hadn't found a replacement for his job at the Breeze Café, perhaps he'd see working for her as a godsend. She'd go by Nick's this afternoon and get the ball rolling.

Sunny felt better and more in control now that she had retrieved her action plan. She got up and stretched, and shuffled to the bathroom. A half-hour later, she was washed and dressed, and ready to face the day.

Sunny headed out to the living room and automatically turned on the television. She always left it on in the background for company. A local tennis tournament was on. She watched the match out of the corner of her eye while she went about straightening up the apartment.

She and Joe used to spend the whole day sitting in front of the TV for the Grand Slam events, stopping only for coffee and bagels in the morning and to prepare buttered popcorn and rum and Cokes when 5 PM arrived. They were both lucky to share this passion. Now she watched it halfheartedly. It just wasn't the same without him.

This mournful thinking about Joe was getting her nowhere. She cherished the 39 years they had together, and now....

Sunny's ears perked up. The commentator was cooing, "Oh, there is Leslie's grandma. She calls her Nan. Isn't she cute?"

She leaned against the vacuum cleaner and focused on the screen. The cameraman had moved in for a close-up of Nan's wide and wrinkled face, watery eyes, and parched lips that were only partially covered with lipstick. She was wearing a paper tiara pinned to the top of shiny white ringlets. The co-anchor replied enthusiastically, "She's adorable. She comes to all of Leslie's matches. "

"Looks like she's been to the beauty parlor for the match," the other surmised.

Sunny was livid. They wouldn't say something like that about the usual significant others who are identified from the crowd: the fiancée with the bright diamond that she positions in camera view by dangling her hand over the side of the players box, or the boyfriend in his preppy sweater and narrow bright tie.

A loud cheer went up from the crowd as Leslie won a point. "Everyone is up on his or her feet, even Gran." The camera once again swung in Nan's direction and caught her just when she was struggling to keep her balance.

"Sure, why not." The other commentator added.

Sunny went over and clicked off the television, fuming about the way older people were portrayed. It was hopeless.

Chapter 31

# Nick

NICK PULLED THE apartment door shut behind him. It was getting harder and harder to leave Mae alone. Just this morning, she seemed to have turned another corner, getting angry about everything. Lately, he'd been feeling tempted to cancel his activities and put his life on hold to take care of Mae, but this meeting with Phil was one that couldn't wait.

The follow-up, after he inadvertently crashed into Mr. Barnes, was surprisingly easy. The ambulance and fire truck came in tandem. The EMT matter-of-factly asked him a few simple questions before moving the body to a stretcher and covering it with a crisp sheet. A few neighbors stood about with an "I've seen this before" look on their faces, but most just glanced quickly their way and then went about their business.

A few hours later, two policemen knocked on Mae's door. They stood in the door jam, interviewing Nick for less than five minutes before snapping their notebooks shut.

Just as they were about to leave, Nick noticed a relatively young couple, probably in their late fifties, walking towards Mr. Barnes's apartment. He had seen them in the elevator a few times before, laden with groceries and a 40-count plastic bag of X/L Depends for Men. They were one of the many children who insisted that their parents move to Regal Crest so they would be in a living situation more conducive to aging.

Nick looked over at them and felt a sudden pang of guilt and sorrow, until he looked more carefully and noticed the relief on their face mixed in with their sadness. In a way, he had done them a favor. He felt his chest swell. He was a good guy, after all.

It was a short bus ride away to the restaurant where he would be meeting Phil, but Nick was running late. He checked his wallet, and sighed at the thought of having to part with six of the few dollars he had left before hailing a cab.

Phil was patiently sitting in a small, semi-closed-off room at the back of the restaurant. It was clear he was a regular here. The waiters were giving him a wide berth for privacy, but at the same time hovering to be at his beck and call if needed.

At the bar was a burly man who had moved the high stool so that he could position himself to see the man in the back room at all times.

Phil was sitting with his hands folded on some stapled papers set on the table in front of him, and appeared to be in the zone.

Nick suddenly felt very shy in approaching him. He still couldn't believe that someone as powerful as Phil would be interested in his project. Nick got close enough to Phil to reach out and pull out a chair to sit in before Phil looked up and acknowledged him.

"Look through this," Phil passed the papers over. "I hope I did your ideas justice."

Nick suddenly felt very nervous. Would he have the balls to say something was wrong if Phil was off-base, or even if something little needed correcting? His mind was spinning so much, it was hard to connect to the reading. He turned on his internal voice; that often worked. "You can do it! You can do it! Just concentrate on the words."

Phil was looking at him quizzically. Nick squirmed in the chair. He wondered how much of his internal struggle was showing on his face and body language. Did he accidentally say some of his thoughts out loud? He tried to summon his inner Lynne and the lessons he learned from his sister. Beads of sweat began to form on his upper lip. His underarms were getting damp, and he could feel a tingling in his crotch.

Suddenly, an idea came to him. He would just pretend he was reading and then say it was okay. How bad could it be? He could go through it with a fine-tooth comb in the privacy of his bedroom later. Yes, he would say that. That would be the responsible, professional thing to do.

Nick let a good five minutes go past, pretending to read but trying to calm his body and mind. When he finally spoke, he was almost back to normal.

"This looks good, Representative Phil." Nick had forgotten his resolve not to use Phil's title so as not to appear in awe of him.

"Call me Phil."

"Okay. Phil. This looks good, but I'd like the time to really look it over before I sign off on it completely." *Let him know that I still have controlling power*, Nick thought. He folded the papers up and stuffed them in his jeans pocket.

"Fair enough. Let me know ASAP. You can do that, right?"

Phil's words made it seem that he was slightly annoyed, but his facial features were calm and serene.

Nick felt he sensed a shift in power. He was losing control, but found himself just nodding his head before blurting out defensively, "Yes, yes, of course."

"Now, for the meat of the issue," Phil leaned in toward Nick until their foreheads almost touched. "How did you do with the homework assignment?"

*What is this? Third grade?* Nick thought as familiar uncomfortable feelings swept through his body.

"It was fine. Mr. Barnes…"

"No need to tell me names."

"Yes. I mean, no… It was easy. It's done." His attempts to off Mae and the accident with Mr. Barnes swept through Nick's mind like a bad movie. He shook his head and body, trying to ward the memories off.

Phil looked at Nick, intently holding a stare.

Nick could feel the heat rising in his skin and a blush on his face. *Does he believe me? Well if he doesn't...* He could have fun thinking about what he would do to Phil. But not here. He'd savor that later for a private recap at home.

"Okay then. Let me outline the rest of the plan... the elimination component. I didn't put any of this in writing for obvious reasons."

Nick tried to compose himself, move away from the dark thoughts about Phil that were sweeping through his mind, and put on what he hoped was his listening face.

"Let's talk about the men gathered for your meeting. It was very clear to me that you were leading up to and just stopped short of suggesting that we end the lives of elderly people. But you just hinted at this, rather than said it directly. That was very smart of you."

Nick found himself grinning widely. He sunk back in his chair, relaxing in the glow of the compliment.

"How many do you think really understood?"

Nick made sure to appear deep in thought, and then shook his shoulders.

"I bet it's not many. You did a really good job packaging what you said. And the ones who think they figured it out will quickly forget once they are offered jobs, money and perks.

"Let's keep this under the radar. You never know when there's a whistleblower in the midst who could ruin everything for everybody. For now, it will just be you and me." Nick didn't know whether Phil was referring to Mike or not, but he had deliberately not invited Mike to this meeting to get the lay of the land first.

Phil knew there were other people he would have to discreetly include in the mix, but there was no need for Nick to know that. It was Nick's idea, true, but he was really just a small player in it all.

"OK," Phil continued. "Listen up. Here's the plan."

Nick found himself sitting up straighter in his chair.

"We have to mix it up. That way, no one can pinpoint an exact age, an exact day, and an exact way that seniors are dying. It has to appear that life is unfolding as normal: that people are dying of natural causes.

"Elimination will take place between ages 70 and 72 so the set cutoff isn't so obvious. The eligibility of a voucher for one's 70th birthday celebration is the trigger that tags a person and puts that individual's plan in motion.

"This has to be done in such a way that things can't be tracked—without a database—hard to do, I know, in this day and age of computers." Phil appeared to be deep in thought, almost talking to himself.

"No one will know when someone will be eliminated and by whom. It will appear as if it just happened, and once it's entrenched into the fabric of society and is part of the norm, people will accept it as part of life and that the same thing will happen to them when their time comes.

"There will be a variety of ways to eliminate people. So far, I've thought of five. I'm sure you'll have some ideas of your own to add." Phil paused, letting his eyes sweep over Nick and connecting with him for a few seconds before continuing. He leaned even closer to Nick and lowered his voice another octave.

"The event will be embedded in the tasks that Regal Crest residents are naturally doing on a day-to-day basis: through the Medical Center, through the restaurants and even grocery shopping; through Rymes Travel excursions, through the shuttle-bus trips, even ironically through fitness activities: golf, swimming, lawn bowling, the exercise room.

"Doctors, restaurant workers, physical trainers, and bag handlers will be given the tasks to do, but they won't know it's part of a bigger plan. When they eliminate someone, they will be given a bonus of some kind, the biggest perk being a job with resources that would have been used for the older person. The reward will be different from time to time so that it's not clear that there's a structured plan. If my memory of Psych 101 serves me right, an unconscious connection will be made between the elimination and the rewards, so it will be repeated automatically. This can work!" Phil leaned back on his chair a smile on his face.

Nick found himself beaming, too. "Darn straight this can work," he mumbled to himself. He had been thinking about this a long time, and as far as he was concerned, that was the understatement of the day.

# Chapter 32

# Nick

The apartment was eerily quiet when Nick entered. Usually by this time, Mae would be roaming through the kitchen, feeling hungry but not quite remembering what she had to do to get something to eat. Nick put his keys on the entry table. "Grandma. Grandma Mae." He walked from room to room. When he got to the room that used to be his grandfather's office, he heard a scraping sound coming from the closet.

"Grandma?" Nick opened the closet door. Mae was crunched in a tiny ball underneath the formal men's suits that hung from the rods, her arms wrapped tightly around her body. Tracks of tears stained her face. Nick crouched down and pulled her over to him, and sat with her head against his chest.

They were still in this awkward position five minutes later. Nick was trying to figure out how to extract himself when the doorbell rang.

"Johnny!" Mae, calling her late husband's name, jumped up, banging her head against the hangers that rattled in place. She rushed across the room, almost slipping on the frayed plaid area rug, down the hallway to the front door. She was fiddling with the locks, a wide smile on her face, when Nick caught up with her. He reached over her and opened the door.

Jane, a neighbor, was standing there, holding a cardboard package in her hands. Mae's face clouded over, and her shoulders slumped as she turned around and shuffled inside.

"This package was sitting right out here. Did you know?" Jane squinted at the label. "It's from FedEx, or maybe UPS." Jane took advantage of the space vacated by Mae and squirmed around Nick to enter the apartment. She put the box on the entry table.

"I've been feeling so lonely. Is this your grandson?" Jane directed her question at Mae, who had plopped down on the sofa and was playing with the buttons on her dress, and appeared not to hear her. Jane settled herself into a chair adjacent to the love seat.

"Nick. I'm Nick."

"Don't worry about me. I'll just sit here a while." Jane's eyes welled up with tears. "I miss him so much. I can't believe it's been eight years. We had a good marriage. He was a good husband to me." She wiped her eyes with the back of her hand. " I just miss him," she whispered. "I wish he were here. It's just not the same. Eight years."

Nick fumbled in his pocket to get a tissue, and when he couldn't find one, he went quickly to the adjacent kitchen to get a napkin. When he came back, Jane was just sitting staring into space with a sad face, and Mae was rocking back and forth.

Nick looked from one to the other and sighed. He was hoping to make a quick turnaround. He had to meet Mike at the bar in a few hours, and he was hoping to have some time to just think things through. Not here—he had no privacy—but perhaps on a park bench. Perhaps he could also take a short snooze. Perhaps… But he still had to make a late lunch for Mae, and it didn't look like Jane was leaving.

"I'll take a glass of water." Jane's request interrupted Nick's thoughts. "On second thought, that's okay. I can get it myself." Jane used her hands to hoist herself off the chair and headed to the kitchen. "Mae's apartment layout is similar to mine." A few seconds later, Nick heard the cabinet door open, then a crash as a glass tumbled to the floor.

# Chapter 33

# Mike

MIKE WAITED AT the bar for Nick. He had picked this place. There was a small round table at the back beyond the pool table where they could talk in private, but for now, he wanted some public time to get himself grounded and smoothed out with a drink.

Mike's feelings were up and down like a roller coaster over the past week. Yes, he was angry. He didn't appreciate the way Nick handled the situation with Representative Phil, who was clearly so full of himself. Would a simple introduction to the Congressman take any skin off his back? But on the other hand, he was sure Nick saw him as his right-hand man. Why else would he have confided all of this in him and had him start the meeting? And he did say he did a good job. But most of all, he was the only one who had the complete picture and the assignment. He was trusted, he was sure. Wasn't he?

Mike sighed. Why was he trying to rationalize all of this? He didn't need this in his life. But there was something almost addictive about it all.

It reminded him of an article he read in the paper about text messaging and waiting for the "ping" of a new message to arrive, or watching the "Steve is writing" notification with bated breath to see what the reply was. It keeps you on the edge of your seat, and this was no different. The adrenaline was running, and he was at the front of it all, not to mention the huge impact he would make. It was hard to walk away from all of this. He must have met Nick for a reason.

As the song went, "time is a healer" and the more time that passed, the more the emotions of the memory faded, and the easier it was to step back and see the big picture. And this was huge. It was worth keeping his cool to be part of this.

Mike went through last week's meeting in his mind again. Yes, it was all okay. He had especially handled his part well. But the assignment part was going to be difficult. Many scenarios ran through his mind, but the answer was KISS. Not the kiss of death—Mike chuckled to himself for coming up with this analogy—but Keep It Simple, Stupid.

This probably would be easier for people who had aging relatives—people they had easy access to. Mike knew nothing about old people. He had no one in his life. His parents died young. He was from a small family. He just couldn't figure it out. He wondered where Nick was in all of this. Had he been able to carry out the deed? He would find out soon enough. He had wanted to get it done before this meeting with Nick. How great it would have been to have it behind him. But there was almost three weeks until the next full meeting. That should be time enough.

On second thought, maybe he should tell Nick he carried out the task even though he hadn't. That was it. Then he would be in the driver's seat. Nick couldn't give him the cold shoulder if he appeared to have some old person's life on the tip of his finger, his hand around their neck.

Mike signaled to the bartender to bring him another shot of whiskey straight up. He had just heard on the news this morning that the brand he drank was being recalled in some countries in Europe because it had an ingredient in it that was also used in antifreeze. *So what?* he thought as the smooth liquid coated his tongue. *You have to go some way.*

Mike looked around him and saw an older man at the end of the bar. He was slumped on the bar stool, his eyes gray, watery and glazed, his face tight and wrinkled, with an empty glass in front of him. His shirt was wrinkled, and Mike could tell that his pants were hiked up around his waist and held in place with a wide buckle. His shoes were scuffed. Mike had seen him here many times before.

*What is his story?* Mike wondered. A month ago, he wouldn't have asked himself that question. The man seemed out of it, lonely and so old. It would be so easy to slide up to him on some pretext to make conversation. He would probably be hungry and eager for small talk. When he looked away, perhaps to signal the bartender for another drink, Mike could easily slip something poisonous in his glass. His head would fall on the counter as he took his last breath. Everyone would assume it would be the drink or age or the loneliness that took him out.

*Yes, that's a plausible scenario*, Mike thought. He could use that with Nick, if Nick asked. That is, if Nick ever got here.

Mike looked at his watch. A half-hour after their meeting time. How annoying and frankly disrespectful is that? Mike signaled to the bartender again, pointing to his glass. He was on his fourth Fireball Whisky before he saw Nick walk through the door.

"Sorry I'm late," Nick sauntered through the door.

*You don't look sorry*, Mike thought, but said, "Hey, that's okay. Gave me a chance to just lubricate up a bit." He gave a half-smile. "I thought that table back there would give us some privacy."

As they walked, Nick continued. "Having problems at home with my grandma. That's why this is so front and center for me."

"Is she the one?" Mike asked.

Nick thought a bit and seemed confused by the question before he got it. "That. Oh. No. I did think about it. I tried. But then another opportunity presented itself."

"Me too," Mike said proudly, and even though it wasn't asked of him, he was surprised to hear his made-up story about taking a senior out spout out of his mouth with great pride.

"So, it can be done," Nick smiled.

They sat with each other quietly for a few minutes in self-satisfaction.

Nick broke the silence. "I had a meeting with Representative Phil this morning."

Mike cringed. Those words were like throwing ice water on what had been a mellow moment. *Why wasn't I invited, dickhead?* Mike thought, but caught himself before the words came out. "Oh. I would have liked to have been there," he said instead, noting that his voice sounded whiny, as if he was pleading.

"Oh, there will be time enough." Nick, unaware of the extent of Mike's angst, dismissed his concerns. "It was a very productive meeting. He took my ideas, expanded them and made everything more specific. Nothing is in writing of course, but..." Nick looked around him and drew his chair closer to Mike. There was something about the intimacy of that action that allayed Mike's concerns somewhat. "Here's The Plan."

Ten minutes later, Nick leaned back in his chair, a satisfied look on his face. "Representative Phil ended by saying, 'This can work' and I thought that's the understatement of the day.

There is no doubt that this can work!" Nick put up his hand to give Mike a high-five.

Mike felt a wave of pleasure as he went skin-to-skin with Nick, and dizzy with the realization that this was only being shared with him. Or was it? The mood was quickly tempered as he imagined Nick and Phil snickering behind his back.

# Chapter 34

# Sunny

It was a long day for Sunny, but she still had one more thing to do: go by Mae's apartment and offer Nick a job. She had meant to get there earlier. Now, she hoped she wouldn't be interrupting their dinner, and that she'd catch Nick before he went out.

There was a lot to do at Regal Crest, and in retirement, for that matter. When Joe was still alive, they had a morning routine: they would watch the 8 AM news together and Joe would freeze the television periodically to rant about what the newscaster was saying. A half-hour show took over an hour to watch at that rate. That was followed by one of two breakfast options that varied day by day—cereal and milk, yogurt with fruit, and of course, the ubiquitous pills and the morning paper. They would take the next few hours to do their own thing, and then had lunch together. Once a week,

Sunny would pick up bacon to go from the Patio Room to make BLTs at home. She was so consistent in doing this that the waitress got it when she came through the door without asking, and she was called "the bacon lady". Sunny would take a 20-minute afternoon nap that sometimes morphed into forty minutes or more. Occasionally, Joe would join her, and they would link fingers as they slipped into a light sleep. Early evening was devoted to rum and Cokes and after dinner, they would watch an hour of TV — a different drama, comedy or reality show each evening.

Sunny missed the ebb and flow of this routine, but when Joe was alive, it sometimes got to her. She understood the adage about not wanting your husband to retire because he would be home all the time and there for lunch. But the single woman on campus has no sympathy for this point of view. In fact, when they saw Sunny and Joe together, they would say that she was lucky to have him. Sunny would think, *He's lucky to have me!* She couldn't imagine that everyone's relationship during their 40 or 50 years of marriage was so perfect. Could it be that none of these Regal Crest husbands had affairs, yelled at their wives, or drank too much alcohol?

Now that Joe was gone, things were different, but it was still a full life for Sunny. In fact, she took pleasure in doing the things she really wanted to do, and not doing the others. Still, at the end of a busy day of meetings, luncheons, concerts or events, when she hadn't touched her to-do list of the mundane things that needed attention, Sunny wondered how she ever got things done when she was working and raising a family, and how her friends, who also had grandchildren in the mix, handled it all. She would give anything for her son to still be alive, dating some girl that he would one day have children with, and make her a grandma.

It was ironic that Mae had Nick, a grandson to dote on and one who was alive to make her a great grandma one day; and she is so out of it, she couldn't appreciate it. Sunny was of sound body and mind, but there was no chance of that happening for her in this lifetime.

Sunny looked through her handbag to make sure the papers she wanted to bring with her were in her purse before heading out the door. She had written up a few notes on what the job for Nick would entail. She consciously picked tasks that would put them in proximity more often than not. It would be hard to delve deeper if they didn't have enough together time to forge a relationship. The job would involve doing handyman tasks in the building she owned; scoping out other condos she could buy as an investment in Regal Crest, and helping her with her end-of-year bookkeeping. He'd have to meet with her for at least two hours a day to get these tasks done.

Fifteen minutes later, she was at Mae's door. She stopped for a minute and took a deep breath. It was strange doing something surreptitious, but it had to be done. She rang the doorbell and waited before ringing again, and then a third time. Many of her tenants had hearing problems, but not Mae. And what about Nick? Sunny looked at her watch: 7

PM. Nick could have gone out, or maybe he hadn't come back yet. She knew how she could find out, although she would be uncomfortable doing so. So many of the older people sat by their windows watching what was going on in the street and parking lot below. Although they wouldn't admit it, other people's activities made up their day.

Sunny knew Nick left Mae alone quite often—more often than he should. She'd have to talk to him about that. Many of the people at Regal Crest were in the same situation. Adult children with young children of their own and work obligations couldn't visit as often as they wanted to or should. The person herself doesn't let on how far gone she is. Sunny saw this quite often with couples. One partner would be disabled and helping the other. The other would be having problems themselves, but would do as much as they could. Sunny remembered reading an advice column that stated, "If you think your parents are having trouble, check to see if there are fingerprints on the wall." She often thought of this when she reached over to pull herself up from a sitting position or balanced against the wall to maneuver a tight space: those telling fingerprints.

But this was strange. By 7 PM, most Regal Crest residents were settled in their homes, caught up in their evening routines—clearing up the dishes from a light supper, watching Vanna White, taking a hot shower, reading a book, and if they were lucky, engaging in a phone call from a child who checked in daily.

It would be especially unusual for someone who was basically home-bound to be out at this time of day.

Sunny rang the bell two more times. Perhaps she should call Nick. She had his cell phone number as an emergency contact in her paperwork. Or perhaps she should enter. She had a set of keys just for emergency purposes. But was this an emergency? It was always hard to figure that out. And was it better to err on the side of caution or the side of privacy? But in this case, with Mae....

Ten minutes later, Sunny was back at her apartment, flipping through her file drawers and rummaging through her stash of keys, looking for the ones for Forest Hill Circle, Apartment 211. By 7:43, she was back outside Mae's door. She rang the bell three more times and put her ear to the door. She could hear the hum of the refrigerator and the tick-tock of a pendulum clock. Something didn't feel right.

She dug deep inside her purse—she had just thrown the keys in willy-nilly—and latched the key ring over her finger. She looked around her, and up and down the hall. She felt very self-conscious and uncomfortable entering the apartment this way. Her hands shook as she put the key in the keyhole. As she turned it to the left, the lock snapped open. Only the single lock was on, so they hadn't locked up for the night yet. Sunny stepped tentatively over the threshold.

"Mae. Nick. Mae." Her voice echoed throughout the apartment. Sunny walked through the vestibule and around the corner into the living room. There was Mae: sitting on the sofa, her head bent in a strange position, slouched to the side. She was dressed in a dark pink business suit. Underneath was a shirt that was also dressy but didn't match—black-and-green paisley. The buttoning was askew. The stockings on her legs had numerous rips, as if she had been frustrated trying to pull them on. On her face were spots of rouge, and her lipstick was drawn across the bottom of her face. Her hands were comfortably folded over a large black patent bag on her lap.

"Mae. Mae," Sunny called as she walked up to her. Clearly, in her mind, Mae thought that she was going somewhere and had made the preparations. Sunny would help her spiffy up a bit or, if she would let her, prepare her for bed.

But as she got closer, Sunny stopped short. "Mae!" she screamed. She put a hand on her arm. Her skin was cold. She then put her finger under Mae's nostril.

Mae was dead.

Chapter 35

# Nick

NICK FELT GREAT. Things seemed so confusing for a while, but now he seemed to have landed in a good place. It was so circumstantial that he was in line behind Mike at the unemployment office and he was able to bring him along. It was nice to have someone he could share this with, especially something as big as this. But an even greater coup was having Phil on board. And Phil got it! Yes, all was good. He'd have to organize a meeting with Phil and Mike, and then they could ramp things up together.

Nick felt like celebrating. He'd bring home a bottle of beer and an all-meat pizza, and just zone out in front of the sports channel with his hand inside his fly. That was his favorite way to relax and unwind.

But just as he was picturing it and planning, he remembered Grandma Mae. God, how could he have forgotten? There was no privacy for that kind of scenario. OK, so he'd make lemonade out of lemons. He would celebrate with Mae. True, she wouldn't have a clue, but wasn't that the plan anyway with all the old people who were going to be part of the program? He chuckled to himself when he thought about her laughing and smiling as they toasted the demise of her contemporaries. She was the lucky one, really, so innocent and too far-gone to feel death creeping up behind her back.

Nick looked at his cell phone. It was 6:30 PM. He still had time. Mae wouldn't need him to help her get ready for bed until 7:30 or 8-ish. He suddenly felt very hungry. It would help to have something coat his stomach after drinking with Mike.

Nick stopped by the Burger King in the plaza near Mae's. It was probably the only fast food joint in the country that had more customers over 80 than young families and children. It was fairly empty at this hour, but there was still a sprinkling of seniors sitting alone around the room. At the back was a group of four senior men. They had coffee, soda cups, and remnants of hamburgers and fries littering the table in front of them; but they were focused on the CNN broadcast on the television screen hung high on the wall near them, and they were talking over each other as they discussed current events.

Many of the seniors coming here for dinner were struggling financially. Nick understood. Since he lost his job, he spent more time here than ever before. With the $.99 menu, a hamburger, fries, salad and a drink—a well-balanced meal, as meals go—could be had for under $4.00. And if a hamburger was all you could afford, partaken with water, and counting the lettuce and tomato on the bun as a vegetable, you could have a meal for under a dollar.

Tonight, there was one kid who appeared to be about six years old jumping around the restaurant, and flitting from table to table. The seniors would look up and smile or wave or beckon for the little boy to come their way. He would come to the table real close before jumping back and laughing. The mother disengaged from her own conversation a few times and signaled the child back. "Don't bother that nice man," she'd say. And the older man would shrug to signal it was no problem at all.

Nick thought about The Plan. A whole generation would go missing. Young people would not have the oldest generation to relate to and to impact their lives.

Nick remembered his own experiences with Grandma Mae and Pop Pop when he was a child and they were younger. Sometimes, his own mother and father were mean and didn't understand him. His father was particularly cruel, especially when he'd been drinking. He would be harsh. Once, he slapped him across the face because he hadn't obeyed fast enough. In his child eyes, his mom just stood back and let it happen. As an adult, he knew that she was probably just scared of him too, but that didn't take the sting off. Once, he heard Grandma Mae try to talk to her daughter-in-law. His mom hung her head in shame, but then fought back. It was her life, and Mae should stay out of it. Besides, her husband was Mae's son. It was her fault that he turned out this way.

Maybe so. His grandparents were such a close-knit couple and so caught up in their own lives, the glamour of roller-skating, and the competition for prizes that they didn't let their son in. They vowed they wouldn't do the same thing with their grandchild.

When his grandparents were around, he would rush into their arms and they would pull him close. He felt safe with them. They were a lot of fun, too—not just caught up in the inertia of day-to-day life.

He loved going roller-skating with them. Roller-skating had always been a part of their lives. His grandparents met at the local roller rink, and it was one thing they had in common that glued them together all of these years. This rink in the neighborhood had longed closed up to make way for a newfangled rec center, part of a wider urban renewal plan. So now, they took the long drive out to a rink near the beach.

Nick loved these outings—sitting with his nose pressed against the window as the crowded landscape gave way to fields and meadows, and then the roller rink itself, with the people, mostly older, who came on a regular basis—the same people every week that he got to know. They would rumple his hair and comment on his gains in roller-skating. It incentivized Nick to get better, and he would practice on his own during the week in the street outside his home.

But then Pop Pop got sick. At first, he thought he was just losing weight. He was proud of his svelte figure. Each week, Grandma Mae would take in his skating outfit, and Pop Pop would proudly show off his new figure. But the weight kept coming off, and his skin began to hang in flabs. Instead of showing off his figure, Pop Pop bundled up to give him the semblance of curves.

It was pancreatic cancer, and once it was diagnosed, it seemed to go downhill from there very quickly. Mae and Pop became one entity, again, in their struggle. They could no longer pay attention to their grandson. Nick stood on the outside, bewildered, not understanding, and feeling hurt and tossed to the side. His parents were also caught up with what was happening with the elders, and no one seemed to care at all about him. Nick stayed on the outside, watching everything change—his anger and resentment and disbelief just boiling up inside.

Mae held it together for only a short while after Pop Pop died. It seemed as if she gave up. She stopped taking care of herself, almost as if inviting death. A few months later, she had a mild heart attack that took her short-term memory away.

Nick pulled out his phone again. It was 7:30. There was a phone number he didn't recognize. Someone had called three times. It was probably a nuisance call; midterm elections were near.

Nick brought his thoughts back to the present. Yes, it would be fun to bring some special food for Mae. Perhaps it wasn't too late to call Cheryl to join him. She always seemed game, even at last-minute invitations like this. He'd check what mood Mae was in before he made a definitive decision about that.

Nick came to Mae's door with two large bags of groceries. He had bought all of Mae's favorite things that he remembered, and some of his own, too—olives, chocolate-covered pomegranate drops, Brie cheese, tonic water, clementines, caramel swirl ice cream. What a combination! He had spent more than he had planned to, but it would be fun.

He was about to put the packages down on the floor to look for his key when he noticed the door was ajar. Strange. He pushed the door open slowly with the tip of his toe, only to see Sunny standing there with her back to him, her phone to her ear.

He was just about to shout out to her, but she must have heard him or sensed him behind her. She turned around quickly and faced him, a pained look on her face, tears rolling down her cheeks.

# Chapter 36

# Sunny

Without thinking, Sunny threw herself into Nick's arms and started sobbing. Nick was still holding the grocery bags, and their sharp edges scratched against her skin. It was only when she felt his body stiffen against hers that she realized how inappropriate her action was, and pulled back.

"I'm sorry. It's just…" Nick didn't seem to notice her. He pushed past her and rushed into the room. He dumped the groceries on the counter and rushed over to Mae. She looked so comfortable there. He sat on the edge of the sofa, gingerly took her hand in his left hand, and unconsciously ran his right hand through her hair. Nick just sat there like that for three or four minutes before eventually collapsing in his chest and letting out a feral groan.

Sunny just stood there, uncomfortable, watching the scene with tears rolling down her face. She was sad: for Mae, for Nick, for herself. At least Mae had Nick to the very end. Who would be here for her? Not Joe. Not Marvin.

Sunny slowly walked up to where Nick was sitting. He didn't seem to notice she was there. Tentatively, she put her hand on his shoulder lightly and just left it there as his groans turned to tiny mews.

* * *

That was two weeks ago. Since that time, Sunny has made tiny inroads into Nick's life. She would even say she was bonding with him in her own way. She's been taking care of him, comforting him like a mother. It was clear to her now that there was no way that Nick could be the bad guy she envisioned. (At least, that's what she thought most of the time.) How could he be when he was so caring to Mae in life, and now, in death?

Sunny helped Nick make his way through the funeral arrangements. Mae hadn't left any directions, so they did something simple: an inexpensive cremation and a small memorial.

Sunny sat at the back of the chapel. There weren't that many people there, but Sunny noticed a young woman come up to Nick, and the wide smile on Nick's face when she tapped his shoulder. She stayed comfortably by his side through the whole ceremony and the afternoon. Sunny was sometimes quick to make judgments, good and bad; and she liked this girl, just from her carriage and attention to Nick. As she watched Nick and Cheryl, she imagined a bright-eyed "grandchild" bouncing on her knee.

Why was she putting herself so seamlessly in the middle of Nick's life? Why was the need and urge coming so fluidly and naturally? It should be because she wants to put herself in a position where she can easily gather more information and find a way to address the happenings she witnessed. But actually, she's tried to put that meeting and all it entailed out of her mind. Is it because she feels sorry for Nick? Is it because she is bored and needs a project in her life? Sunny tossed these around in her mind, but knew that the truth is it all comes back to Marvin. It was funny that after all this time, she can't let go and is recreating the closeness by building this relationship with Nick and by being a mother again.

Sunny thought about this as she made her way over to Mae's apartment for the second time that day. She's allowed Nick to stay a month rent-free to give him time to make plans. She even set up an office space in Mae's dining room for Nick to use, put him on the payroll, and gave him some small tasks to do to help her with her rental business: setting up spreadsheets to keep track of income and expenses for the IRS, and some building maintenance tasks. It feels nice to have someone to share this with, however fleeting and temporary.

Now she was going to tell Nick that she had arranged to have the apartment painted in a few days so she could begin showing it to a new tenant. Nick would have to be away on that date. She could have just called and told him over the phone, but she needed an excuse to see him again. The house painting would be an opportunity to search Nick's desk and computer again. She'd be doing it just because she has the opportunity. She didn't expect to find anything. Now she felt guilty just thinking about it!

# Chapter 37

# Nick

NICK STOOD IN the middle of Grandma Mae's apartment and looked around him. It was a mess. It was so easy when he was keeping the apartment in tiptop shape for Mae. He had no choice. Anything that wasn't where it was supposed to be would throw Mae off, and who knew what her mind would tell her to do? She might end up putting the TV remote in the refrigerator, thinking it was something edible if it wasn't right next to the television, where it belonged.

You'd think that knowing Sunny was dropping by so often would give him the impetus to keep the rooms fairly neat, at least. He started to do that at first. But Sunny didn't seem to mind, and so he paid less attention to it as the days wore on. She would stop by, and as they were chatting, her hands would be busy, almost mindlessly straightening up whatever was around her. She didn't seem to judge him.

Nick surveyed the room again. *That may be so*, he sighed, *but this time things looked too grungy even for his own sensibilities.*

Nick was surprised at how much he missed his grandmother. There was a hole in his life now that she was gone. But often, a wash of relief would come over him, and he would feel guilty again that he wanted her gone. He couldn't even say that she is better in this other place. She had no idea of anything during the end of her life. She was there already.

And this connection with Sunny was also a surprise. But he was just letting it happen. He enjoyed these last two weeks with Sunny. Most importantly, he noticed that his headaches and the voices in his head were waning. It was nice to be cared for, being the recipient rather than the giver. He had been caring for Mae for so long that except for brief interludes with Cheryl, and that was a sexual thing, he forgot what it was like. And there's nothing like a mother's caring and unconditional love, which is what he was getting from Sunny.

Ironically, Nick was in the best position he'd been in for a while. Sunny was letting him stay rent-free while he settled Mae's affairs. She had given him some odd jobs to do, and was basically giving him a free hand to figure out how to modernize her record-keeping system electronically, even setting up a place in Mae's dining room for him to work. This arrangement gave him regular income coming in, if only temporarily. In addition, when he went through Mae's belongings, he found wads of money stuffed here and there throughout the house. When he added it up, he had more than $3,000 in cash. That was nice pocket change.

Nick was putting the last piece of garbage in the trash and wiping off the kitchen counter when the phone rang. He looked at the screen. Phil was calling again. He had been calling a couple of times a day for the past few days. Mike had been calling, too. Nick had been ignoring the calls. He thought that having to attend to Mae's funeral arrangements would be a good excuse. He wished they would just go away. He wished he had never started all this political stuff. Radical solutions—that seemed like the right thing to do at the time.

He looked at Phil's number again and clicked the redial icon. He broke out in a slight sweat while he listened to it ring.

"Well, it's about time." That tone of voice made Nick feel like a bad son.

"It's just…"

"I know… my sympathies. Ha! Ha! You of all people know that's for the best."

"Yes, I guess." Nick could feel himself rising to a boil as conflicting thoughts crashed through his mind. Up front and center was how someone that cold and heartless should be taken out.

"No guessing about it! Pull yourself together. We've got work to do. Let's meet this evening for an early supper at Ruby's."

"I have to… I mean, I want to bring Mike with me."

"Mike?" Phil left a long pause. "Oh, Mike. OK. I'll see you both then."

Nick opened his mouth to reply as he heard a click in his ear. He looked at the phone in disbelief as he felt a mild headache swelling on his right lobe. It was a nightmare. He'd call Mike right away to let him know, and then he could put this behind him for a few hours.

He was waiting for Mike to pick up when he heard Sunny at the door. Nick walked over with his phone to his ear and opened the latch. He waved her in.

Sunny stepped in and stood uncomfortably in the foyer. She didn't mean to eavesdrop, or did she?

"Mike. We're meeting with Phil this evening at Ruby's. How about if we get together first, around 4 PM? I want to have everything planned so we can be in control of what's happening. OK, great!"

Sunny busied herself with taking off her coat and putting her pocketbook and briefcase on the kitchen counter. She was dreading this day. It sounded like after all this time, something was moving along. And it didn't sound like a good thing. Not at all.

# Chapter 38

# Sunny

SUNNY WAITED PATIENTLY for Nick to get off the phone, then gave him a piercing look. "Sounds like that was important."

Nick looked at Sunny sheepishly. He felt some color rising in his face, and the headache getting sharper. He'd been enjoying these two weeks with Sunny, but who was she to judge? He tightened his fist, then took a deep breath and relaxed it finger by finger. He knew he was overreacting.

"Nah, but I have to get back to my own responsibilities and routines at some point. I just wish it wasn't now." Nick gave a hollow laugh.

"I'm glad I had the time to help you out, though," Sunny said. "I still can't believe Mae is gone. You'd think I'd be used to it. People die all the time, especially in a community like this. And you've been a big help to me."

Sunny looked up at Nick, and noticed he seemed more relaxed. "Anything else you need to tell me about the spreadsheets?" she asked.

Two hours later she was heading home with a draft of the spreadsheet and detailed instructions on how to use it. She'd forgotten a lot of what Nick said already. That's one thing she didn't like about getting old: keeping up with all the newfangled things, especially technology. But she was better than most people at Regal Crest. Thanks to her weekly classes, she had enough basic knowledge of computers to feel comfortable; and she was getting pretty good at using a smart phone, too.

Nick seemed disappointed when she told him she would be having the house painted tomorrow to get it ready for a new tenant. She was sure he was hoping he could stay there longer. She had been looking the other way. Having someone to watch after Mae and make sure she didn't cause any trouble outweighed the rule that you needed to be 55 or older to live in Regal Crest. But now, she needed to tighten things up again before others saw this as an excuse for them to disregard the rules. People didn't mean to be bad. They just looked out for themselves.

# Chapter 39

# Mike

It seemed to Mike that he was always the one waiting for Nick. He was becoming a fixture in this bar.

Nick had called him, staying on the line only for a few seconds to tell him his grandmother had died, and he'd get in touch with him shortly. That was two weeks ago, and Mike felt dissed. Mike couldn't understand what the big deal was, and the crocodile tears when this was obviously part of The Plan. Nick was good. Mike was green with envy that Nick had taken care of two people and he'd done none. That should put Nick in good stead with Representative Phil, and then where would he be? At least Nick didn't blink when he told him his made-up story of who he offed. It must have sounded plausible.

Mike had been calling Nick, almost desperately toward the end, to make sure things weren't moving forward without him; and now one call, and the anxiety was gone. His body was calm and peaceful. He was worried that Nick and Phil were bonding and leaving him out, and that Nick never intended to introduce him to Phil. He tried to rationalize—he didn't care; he didn't need them in his life. But his body was tied up in knots. Now Nick was plotting strategy with him before the meeting with Representative Phil, and he'd been invited. They'd put their heads together. All was suddenly good with the world.

* * *

Five minutes later, Nick strode in. It took him awhile for his eyes to adjust and to move through the bar, giving Mike a chance to give him the once-over. He appeared jittery; his face was pinched. Mike wondered what that was all about, but just filed the impression at the back of his mind.

"Hi." Mike stood halfway up to shake Nick's hand, but sat back down again when it wasn't offered. "How'd it go?"

"How'd what go?"

"You know."

"Actually, I don't know," Nick replied sourly.

This wasn't going as well as Mike expected.

"Your grandmother. You're lucky. I don't have any old relatives. It's easier in a way with people, you know. Especially since we know that what we're doing is the best thing. It's easier than with a stranger." Mike felt he was going on and on.

Nick felt the blood start pounding behind his ears and put his head on his hand. "I didn't do it. She died a natural death."

"Right." As soon as that sarcasm came out of his mouth, Mike wondered if he had gone too far.

Nick gave Mike a cold stare.

"It doesn't matter. As far as anyone knows, you did two. That's very impressive. Representative Phil will be impressed."

"I don't know if I care." Nick emitted a long, audible sigh.

"You can't give up on this. It is too important. Besides, look at the people who are now involved. I can't do this on my own."

"I'm not asking you to."

They both sat there, just staring at each other for a moment or two. This was so different from the magnetic camaraderie they had when they first met.

Finally, Nick broke the ice. "It's just that this has been really hard for me. I know I didn't return your calls or anything. I didn't expect to feel this way."

"It's hard doing something like killing another person. It's hard to be cold-hearted. There's regret to contend with, if you're any kind of human being." *What, am I a psychologist?*

Mike thought, surprised at the words coming out of his mouth.

"I told you, it wasn't me."

"Just a coincidence, then. Your grandma finally dies, just at the point when you're considering an elimination program for senior citizens. You can tell me." Mike didn't know why he was being so hard on Nick. He just felt so angry about being left hanging out to dry all these past days.

Nick pushed himself up from the table. "I don't have to put up with this. I'm getting the support I need from others. I don't really need you and your half-assed sympathy."

"Wait!" Mike unconsciously put his hand up to Nick, and Nick coiled backward. "I'm sorry."

Nick paced around the table and sat down again. He looked Mike over. "Let's try again."

They sat silently. Nick was in a meditative state. Mike's eyes darted and his body squirmed.

Finally, Nick broke the silence. "We'll be meeting with Phil in a few hours. I like him. I think he'll be helpful to our cause. But I also think he has an agenda of his own, and will more than take the lead on this. He'll take over, if he can. He sees us as amateurs in the political arena. We probably are, but so what? We have passion, and this is so much bigger than the three of us. We can decide how we want to use him. Let's go through the steps again to be sure everything is airtight."

Mike's mind was racing. *Yay! Yay! Yay! Nick is willing to put Representative Phil in his place.* Mike loved how he was feeling now. It's amazing how quickly moods can change.

# Chapter 40

# Phil

P HIL GOT TO the restaurant early. He always did. It was important to stake out a quiet area for meetings such as this. This was his first time at this restaurant. He didn't want to go to his usual haunts. It was important not to be predictable or be easy to locate after.

More often than not, he would be recognized, and the assumption would be made that he needed a quiet corner and he'd be led there. But today, he tweaked his look at little bit—just enough that while there might be a question in someone's mind, it wouldn't be enough to put two and two together. But if you knew who you were looking for, it would be easy to find him, and that's what Phil expected of Nick and Mike.

Phil had been involved in many things as a Representative over the years, things that were impactful and that he was very proud of. But he had a good gut feeling about this one. It was going to trump it all. He'd bet anything he was right, and was willing to put it all on the line.

He pulled out four copies of the chart he had developed and stacked them to his right. Then he looked in his briefcase for the latest Grisham novel. He was so involved in reading, he didn't hear or see Nick and Mike when they came in. They were standing uncomfortably over him, waiting for him to acknowledge that they were there.

"Oh, there you are." Phil didn't bother to get up from his seat or to shake their hands. He just waved to the empty seats around him for them to sit down. He had positioned himself so that one man would have to sit on one side of him, and the other on the other. That came in handy when he wanted to cut someone out of the conversation to make them feel little and unimportant.

Phil cut right to the chase. He turned his face and his piercing eyes on Mike first. "How did it go? How did it feel?" He noted that Mike squirmed slightly in his seat, and that a pink flush spread up his neck beneath the colorful macho tattoos.

"You're talking about…?" Mike was trying to bide time.

"Yes!"

"Well, er…"

Phil cut Mike off impatiently. "On second thought, spare me the details. You're here, aren't you?"

"Well, for me, it was surreal." The words spilled out of Nick's mouth, partly to deflect the scrutiny on Mike, and partly in defense of himself for including Mike in the meeting. "At first, I thought I couldn't do it and then boom, it was easy." Nick felt that strange emotion fill up inside of him. "Pow! Pow! Pow!" Nick formed a gun with his fingers, pointing it at Phil and then quickly pointing it at Mike before, embarrassed, unfolding his fingers. He hung his head. He didn't have to look to know that Phil was looking at him like he had two heads.

"Okay then." Phil paused a long time to let his disappointment at Mike's inarticulateness and Nick's strange behavior resonate. "So, the good thing is now, we have three less people dependent on the government and draining money from us." Phil knew about Mae's passing. He also knew that by including her in the number count, he was just inches short of saying, "Your Mama."

Under the table, Nick balled his hand into a fist, then released it.

"What about the others? Can we bring them in? Do you think they'd be able to handle an assignment like this? Should we use it as our test?" Phil pretended he was thinking out loud. "No, based on how you both handled this…"

*Is he thinking 'You idiots'?* Nick wondered, and glanced at Mike to see if he was processing it the same way. *Phil has no idea what I had to mentally go through to kick myself into gear to complete this task.* Anger took over Nick's thoughts. Mike just sat stiffly in his seat, as if he were wishing he could be anywhere but here.

"Based on that, I think we should give out assignments, but without people really knowing what they are doing." Phil continued, seemingly oblivious to what Nick and Mike were feeling. "As I said to Nick when we met a few weeks ago, the beauty of it is that at 60, 70, 80 and up, older people die naturally so no one will think anything is up. So, if a few people die after eating a Western omelet at the Regal Crest restaurant, no one will assume they've been poisoned. And if a couple of people get hit crossing the street, they'll assume it's one of the bad Regal Crest drivers. If the pharmacist gets the prescription wrong, as long as it's spaced to happen sporadically, they'll assume it's one more old person reacting to his medicine. But at the same time that you are clearing out people who are already over 70, you are setting the expectation for those approaching this age. Now here are my suggestions on how we should structure the meeting."

Nick disconnected from what Phil was saying. *This is really going to happen,* he thought. He was proud. But how did control slip out of his hands? When did this become Phil's baby instead of his? He should inject something into the planning, something brilliant. But shit, he hadn't been listening just now. He lost the thread. Mike was just sitting there, looking so subservient. Why couldn't he do something to turn the tide? Mike knew the ropes almost as much as he did!

"What do you think, Nick?" Phil's tone let Nick know that he was asking just because he thought he had to.

"OK, I guess."

"I guess? Think about what we're saying. What we're doing is just natural steps from what you outlined."

"I see that," Nick said angrily.

"OK. We're done here." Phil gave copies of the chart to Nick and Mike, picked up his novel, and stuffed it into his bag. "We're all set for our next meeting as far as I am concerned… Good to go. Later, guys." Phil didn't look back as he strode out of the room, waving left and right to random people as he passed their tables. He knew the impact his cutting everything off would have.

Nick looked across at Mike. He was just noticing how Mike's face changed colors with his emotions. No wonder he was picked on as a child. Now it was an ashen white with a pale-yellow undertone.

"OK. So, what now?" Mike asked. "Who does he think he is?"

Nick smiled a slow smile across his face. "He doesn't know shit! We've got it." He put up his hand to give Mike a limp high-five.

# Chapter 41

# Sunny

SUNNY MADE UP her mind. It would be easier to snoop among Nick's stuff now that he was halfway on her payroll and doing computer work for her. She could say she was looking for the latest spreadsheet if Nick walked in on her or if he noticed that something was awry. The painter's visit would be the perfect opportunity. She could even say she had to move things around, so the painters could more easily get to the walls, if it came to that. She hated acting surreptitiously, like she didn't trust Nick, when it was more to confirm that her gut instinct was right: that Nick wouldn't be involved in something so bad.

The next morning, first thing upon awakening, Sunny scanned her mind for unfinished business. The snooping resolve came up, and it still felt right to her. She'd feel more comfortable fostering a relationship with Nick if these question marks were resolved.

But first, her morning routines. The day always felt better if she followed the series of things that her doctors expected of her or magazines say are good for her health and longevity. The list was getting longer and longer. She had to monitor it so that it didn't get so cumbersome that she would just give up on it all. After all, there was a balance between doing what was needed to keep you at your best and doing so much that you couldn't enjoy life.

She started with stretching in bed. She found that by getting out the kinks, something as simple as walking was easier. Then she journaled. She kept a gratitude journal where she wrote down the five things she was grateful for. On some mornings, it was difficult to complete the list. She would sit on the edge of the bed, tugging at her mind, trying to fill the fourth or fifth point, and nothing came to her. Then she would feel sorry for herself. Nevertheless, she would be sure to complete the list, even if all she could think to say was "I woke up today."

Then she did some floor exercises—a combination of a yoga routine and a series of exercises from physical therapy. She had been to so many physical therapy sessions for so many reasons that she couldn't keep up, but it helped keep everything at bay. She used to do mat exercises on the floor, but now it was difficult getting up and down. Her doctor said, "Do it anyway. Once you stop practicing, what are you going to do if you fall down and get stuck on the floor? You won't know how to get up." But try as she might, it was too hard to do now. She just hoped that she would be the lucky one and that wouldn't happen to her. Then there was the medicine routine. Sunny made sure to follow the doctor's instructions exactly. There were others she knew who cut corners or made their own decisions around meds, but not Sunny.

Sunny was glad she was living at this time of life when there were so many options for good health. As much as she complained about all the medicine she was taking, she was living in a time when there were ways to cure, treat, or put an illness in remission so people could live a full life. And Medicare. She hadn't thought about it until she was 65, but what a blessing! She sat by the television during the debates on Obamacare, wishing it would be a single-payer system, Medicare for All, so that everyone could have the comfort of a safety net like she had and not have to worry about how they would pay for medical costs. She was especially lucky— Joe had an excellent plan. Her Medicare Part B and out-of-pocket expenses were paid through his union.

Her breakfast routine was the same healthy meal every day—yogurt, granola, fruit, sunflower seeds, bananas; or if she was in a rush, kefir and toast. Then she went out for a walk.

Walking was a pleasure here. In the other places Sunny lived in, she was always looking over her shoulder to see what was coming up behind her. Here, she felt safe.

There were always a number of people walking along the Boulevard. Some of the same ones walked day after day. It was inspirational. One was a woman in her nineties who was so bent over, her nose almost touched her knees. She was out every day, in the same scarf and jacket, pushing herself around on a walker. But Sunny hadn't seen her lately. At Regal Crest, she knew what that probably meant.

All the walkers would say hello or good morning as they passed. Well, almost everyone. Joe used to get upset if someone didn't reply. He thought he was deliberately being snubbed. But Sunny would just laugh. "Half the people here can't see; the other half can't hear. Give them the benefit of the doubt."

Sunny was so glad she got to Regal Crest when she did. The ads for senior living facilities always had people saying, "I wish we had gotten here sooner", and it was true. Most people got here in their eighties; but by then, it was too late to have a physical exercise routine, be it walking, tennis or golf. Sunny was also glad she had a chance to make friends while Joe was alive. That made the transition to living alone much easier.

Sunny made it to the apartment at 8:30 AM, just as the painters were arriving. She had used them many times before, and would have been comfortable even if they had started without her. They put drop cloth over the furniture in the living room and started to head toward the dining room where the office was set up, but Sunny stopped them and told them to wait until they were ready—she had some work to do there. She slipped into the ergonomic chair behind the desk that she had found on sale at IKEA, and looked around. Her ears were perked. She heard the hum of the painters chatting, the clicking of the brushes, the news report on the radio, but kept her mind on listening for a door slam or footsteps that would indicate Nick was back.

What luck! Piled on the corner of the desk were some papers—notices and flyers—that looked like they came from a meeting.

Sunny took them and began to fold them to put in her bag, but then stopped. On second thought, it would be better if Nick didn't know she saw them or that they were gone. She had time. She would patiently go through the notes and then commit them to memory.

An hour later, Sunny signaled for the painters to come in. If they had known her, they would have been surprised to see the change in her face and carriage. She was determined, and she had made up her mind. She'd go to this next meeting. It would be easier without Mae in tow.

# Chapter 42

# Nick

For the past few days, Nick hadn't been feeling it. His bravado with Mike after Phil left them at the meeting seemed like a long-ago dream. He was just hunkered down in his freshly painted apartment—so clean and pristine—thinking about the next person who would be living here. It hit him that it wouldn't be him. His connection to Sunny, his feeling good about taking this social issue in hand, his feeling that he was cared for was all a fantasy.

Sunny had let him be for the past few days. Maybe she was feeling guilty about kicking him out. She said she would still have work for him. But his current behavior would probably make it difficult for her to follow up on this.

And it was getting harder and harder being the sweet Nick and not letting the other side come out. It was scary.

Sometimes, he watched himself from a distance, like when he put the finger gun up in Phil's face. What was he thinking?

The last thing he said to Mike is "We got it," but now he was thinking, "We got what?" Nothing had changed. Nick had done nothing this past week. How did he end up here in his sweats and undershirt for three days in a row, unshaven? He'd have to make an effort and pull himself together for the meeting tomorrow.

Nick went over to the papers on his desk. Is this the way he left it? He was sure he had put it in two stacks. He thought for a minute and pushed the question out of his head. *This is good*, he thought, as he flipped through the papers. He picked up a red pen and began making margin notes.

# Chapter 43

# Phil

P HIL WALKED TO the front of the makeshift meeting room, storage boxes lining the side, and looked out over at the men sitting around the rectangular table in front of him: twelve people in total, the same number who had been at the first meeting. He had the original roster, and checked it again and again. It was right, but it didn't matter. He had placed all the names in his memory bank.

Nick had just given a short introduction to the meeting, welcoming everyone back and pumping them up. Then according to the agenda, it was his turn to speak, and then Nick would come out again. But Phil knew it wasn't going to happen that way. He had deliberately left Mike off the agenda. Yes, he knew that Mike took the lead at the last meeting when Nick was late, but that didn't have to mean that it would always be that way. Mike had positioned himself at the back of the room, and from his body language, Phil could tell he was fuming. *Just where I want him.* Phil briefly sported an internal smile before repositioning his face again.

"Hi. For those of you who don't know me, I'm Phil Richards, Representative of District #26. I am very excited about this project, and honored to be part of this committee and action plan. I have a lot to offer. I can act as a liaison between your group and the powers-that-be in the government.

"We're going to start where we left off at the last meeting. First, I'm going to pass around a summary sheet which describes The Plan in more detail." Phil walked over to give the handouts to the man seated on his far left so they could be passed around. "I'll give you a few minutes to read it, and then I'll answer your questions." Phil took a seat up front and waited. He felt like a college professor.

Five minutes later, he glanced around the audience. Most of the men were looking up. A couple were fiddling with their cell phones. "Does anyone need more time?" Phil locked eyes with each one by one and thought, *If they knew what was coming next...*

A man in a denim shirt raised his hand. "I read in the paper the other day that 40% of the budget goes to Social Security and Medicare. That doesn't leave much for us."

"This makes things fairer." The man who had the floor waved the handout over his head. "Imagine what we could do with that extra money. But I think my grandfather would keep it all to himself."

"But streamlining the system can't hurt," a third man chimed in.

Phil's cell phone rang. He looked at it, and a wave of concern came over his face. "Excuse me for a minute," he said, walking to the door with his cell phone, then turning back to get his iPad and notes, too. Once he was a few feet away from the meeting room, he picked up his pace so much that the walking almost became a run. He didn't notice Mike following him at a close distance.

Just when he rounded a corner, a huge explosion shook the building behind him. Phil's body flinched, but he didn't look back just kept moving swiftly away from it all.

# Chapter 44

# Sunny

Sunny's resolve was so strong when she had decided to go to this meeting. But now she was questioning herself. Did she really have to delve this deeply into Nick's life? How many people in her life had she been close to, yet knew nothing about? Not knowing everything about someone, in many cases, didn't even get in the way of forming a deep relationship.

When did retirement get to be so complicated? Gladys, her neighbor down the hall, had a simple routine. Gladys' daughter dropped off the grandchildren each morning. Sunny would look out the window and see Gladys pushing a stroller with the older child, and the baby strapped to her chest. Sometimes, you would see a pacifier or a small toy lost on a road in Regal Crest, and it seems an anomaly until you remembered everyone's grandchildren visiting.

Another neighbor, Carolyn, did volunteer work that filled her day—at the Regal Crest library and for the local botanical garden. But Sunny always thought that this kind of regimented activity would feel like going to work. Sure, she signed up to help as part of the movie committee, but that was time-limited.

Others visited the sick and the home-bound or delivered meals on wheels, but those tasks were too depressing for Sunny. She didn't need a window into where she would eventually be heading.

But today was bigger, and by far more complicated. In her heart, Sunny knew she was in the middle of something big. All she had to do was unravel it. If she understood it correctly, there would be big changes in store for seniors put in place by younger people who didn't understand. She hadn't understood aging herself. In fact, she might not know the nitty-gritty of those directly ahead of her—those in their 80s and 90s. Parents don't talk to their kids about this. But one 80-year-old summed it up this way: "It sucks," he said.

Sunny thought about Mae. Today was like déjà vu all over again; but last time, she had Mae with her. She remembered how stressed out she felt having to take her along with her, and Mae giggling in the middle of the meeting. But it was kind of fun having her along. It was lonely now.

Sunny snapped out of her reverie. This side trip down memory lane was going to make her late for the meeting, and she might not be as lucky in being able to slip in this time.

It took a while to catch a cab. And she remembered to have the driver drop her off at a Starbucks a few blocks away. She knew she should probably be rushing to get there, but decided to stop and use the bathroom and get a cup of coffee. It was better to come in after everyone had settled in, anyway. Sunny realized she was procrastinating because she felt so uncomfortable, but she pushed that to the back of her mind.

Ten minutes later, Sunny was walking toward the building. Sometimes, she had to be careful with her balance as she walked, and today was one of those days. If someone passed too close to her it caused her to sway, and she had to take baby steps to catch her footing.

That's why she noticed the man rushing past her in the other direction as she was within a block of the building. He was so close. He was dressed in dark clothing but was sporting a red tie, like what politicians often wear. *That must be why he looks familiar*, Sunny thought, the red tie ringing a bell for her. *He must be someone I've seen on CNN.*

Boom! There was a loud sound, followed by the streaming slide of crumbing brick and wood. Dust began to rise and spread through the street.

As she walked, Sunny's mind was so intent on solving the puzzle of who the man who almost bumped into her was that it took a minute to bring herself back to the present moment.

She stopped her forward motion and flattened herself against a wall. The building she was about to enter was engulfed in flames. Suddenly, what was once a door frame was pushed down, and a man came running out. His shoulder and shirt were singed, and as he passed Sunny, she could see colorful tattoos melting with the skin on his arms.

"Nick!" Sunny looked at the building in horror. People had started gathering around at a distance. The sirens of fire trucks started blurring, and getting louder and louder. There was no movement from the building, just the licking sounds of flames punctuated by sirens.

"Nick!" Tears were silently rolling down Sunny's face. Unconsciously, she started moving towards the blast.

Someone reached out and pulled the edge of her jacket. "Where are you going? Stop right here, grandma." A strapping guy stepped out of the crowd and pulled her close to him.

Sunny strained to get away, but in a moment of lucidity, she thought, *What am I doing? Even if Nick survived this, I wouldn't want him to know I was here.* She didn't want to be remembered by this guy, either. No problem. Old people were invisible and slipped through the cracks. Each old person looked like the other.

The enormity of what this all meant hit Sunny like a ton of bricks. She might be the only one who knew what was going on. It's a good thing she had that paperwork to back up what they were doing.

In fact, where did she put the paperwork? It must be somewhere at home. And then Sunny remembered. She had decided at the last minute not to take the paperwork. She didn't want to tip her hat to Nick. She had committed it to memory. Sunny closed her eyes and scrunched her face, willing the information to come up front and center. But try as she might, nothing triggered anything. She had forgotten it all.

# Chapter 45

# Nick

*S*O, THIS IS *what it was like.* Sheer terror sliced through Nick's mind as he heard the blast and felt the terrible pain in his body. Then his life flashed before his mind, from the tears at childbirth to tying his shoes this morning.

This had happened to him twice before, in bright technicolor: once when he flew over the handle rail of a motorcycle, and another time when he was sleepwalking and gashed his head in a bad fall when he was trying to get back into bed.

But this time was different. There was so much pain. He didn't have to put his hand against his body to feel the blood flowing out. It was sticky and gooey and made his clothes feel like tourniquets against his body.

Although he was standing near the front of the room, the blast threw him back into the crowd, and dropped him twisted and contorted. Nick could not move his head or body, but could sense someone very close to him and feel his low groan.

So, this was it. It was a silly way to go, and the timing sucked. His taking care of Mae and growing relationship with Sunny were beginning to give him a new perspective on life. He wouldn't use the word "enjoy," not yet, but he was beginning to accept and feel mellow with the rhythm of taking care of Mae. She was like a loyal dog, there for him when he came home and so trusting. And now, he was feeling cared for by Sunny. Cheryl cared for him too, but in a different way. There was always the underlying demands of sex, the back-and-forth and compromises of a relationship with Cheryl. With Sunny, it was just there, no strings attached.

Well, it was too late now. Nick's mind turned back to Cheryl. Would she miss him? Would she get into another relationship right away? He hadn't been with her long enough to have any expectation. Once, he heard Sunny and her friends debating the five-year rule and how it seemed that when someone's wife died, they were in a new relationship within weeks or months, even if they'd been with their wife for over 50 years. "What am I, chopped liver?" the friend had asked. Nick had just listened to this and laughed. Who knew that complicated issues like this were going on in a senior community?

Nick twisted his legs, trying to unwrap them from the painful position he was in. He felt the life slipping from his body. Who would have thought the last minutes of his life would be spent thinking about such mundane stuff? But it kept his mind off of his excruciating pain. *Yes, I had a brilliant mind,* Nick thought. *But look where it got me. I never used it to my advantage.* He wondered what would have happened if he had been given more time to live. Would he have married Cheryl, perhaps had a son, little Nick? He reached out to the sweet, innocent child his mind had conjured up, but the boy started to fade away.

The pain was making it too painful to think, and thinking was painful, too. Nick dropped little Nick's hand, gave in to the physical pull of his body, and closed his eyes.

## Chapter 46

# Mike

MIKE ROLLED OVER in bed. The momentum almost pulled him over the edge. He opened his eyes. As happened every morning, the events of the last few weeks flooded through his mind. When he wasn't sleeping, he was lying wide awake as he waded through the muck of memories all night long. It was exhausting, but this too would pass.

He put on his slippers and robe, and shuffled to the door. This had become his morning ritual—getting the paper even before peeing. He made sure his robe was hanging in such a way that it would cover his arm tattoos before opening the door. The things you don't think about when getting a tattoo are funny, like the fact that branding makes it easier for people to recognize you. Mike flipped through the newspaper pages. There was nothing. They were on to different things, and had been since a few days after the event.

Mike had been lucky. He hadn't been part of the meeting, or at the front of the room. Mike was pissed. It was clear that Phil was trying to squeeze him out. When he was given the handout with the agenda, he was livid. Nick was on first, followed by Phil, followed by Nick again.

But there was something in the way the agenda was worded that seemed wrong to Mike. It was so focused in the beginning, but seemed to fall apart in the second half. And then halfway through the meeting, Phil picked up his iPad, notes, and phone; and started heading to the exit. Mike decided to follow him, but Phil was huffing it out, and it was hard to keep up.

Just as he crossed the threshold out of the building, the blast went off. Mike's body was slammed against an adjoining wall. For a second, everything went blank. When he came to again, he quickly looked around him, but Phil was gone.

Mike stood across the street, waiting to see if anyone else came out, but no one did. Shortly after, there were sirens and ambulances; and minutes later, stretchers with sheets draped over body forms. Mike could almost feel a sheet tighten over his nostrils. That could have been him. He stood there numb, his body pounding with alternate waves of nausea and tsunamis of relief.

Now, Mike put the newspaper on top of the file cabinet in his sparsely furnished room, and out of habit, pulled the handle of the bottom drawer to make sure it was locked. No one would be looking for his papers and notes, evidence that this even happened, but it was best to be careful.

In fact, why was he saving it? Because... Well, you never know, it could come in handy one day. No one knew that he had it, or that he had been part of this, or was alive for that matter, certainly not Phil. Phil had smugly walked away, thinking he had cleared the deck. Mike had been so angry at how Phil blew him off, but now he realized he was lucky that Phil hadn't made the effort to get to know him. It was all so stupid: the flattery, the bravado, the weak moment in the employment line when he was smitten by Nick and impressed by his ideas.

Mike felt a rare flush of happiness and flood of relief. Yes, he would put this out of his life. The truth was that he had dodged a bullet. It was done.

Chapter 47

# Sunny

SUNNY WOKE UP to another gloomy day inside and out. Sometimes, the sunrise filtered through the leaves and made a beautiful, dappled pattern backdrop from her window. Not today.

It was like losing Marvin again, only worse. When Marvin died, she had her husband Joe in a way. He had his own struggles he was going through, but he was a physical presence there, on a parallel path. And much of her energy was spent consoling him so he wouldn't feel as badly as he did—not that it helped. And then by the time Joe died, she'd been expecting it to happen. She had a long lead-in. Prostate cancer can be a slow death.

After Joe died, people came to visit. She hated to say it, but some of the people at Regal Crest were professional mourners. Good for them; it was something for them to do.

And good for her and the other people who were suffering and were helped by their support.

But no one knew of Nick or her connection to him. No one knew of her fantasy of having Nick as a Marvin substitute. No one knew of Nick's secrets that she was keeping.

Nick's family swept in and out. She had seen a few at Mae's funeral, but it seemed that only death brought people out. It was amazing how much support you got to put final affairs in order. People saw her just as Nick's landlord and part-time boss. They were congenial enough for a few seconds, and then just dismissed her.

Sunny wondered what people who had secret affairs did. They were an important part of their lovers' lives, but no one knew of their existence. She was lucky she never had to doubt Joe in that way. Sunny sometimes wondered about the perfect couples at Regal Crest. Were they always that way, or did old age send the straying partner home to roost?

Sunny heard a loud, persistent, almost angry knock on the door. It was 11:17 AM, and she was still in bed. She rolled over and swung her feet over the side. Her cell phone was beeping, and the light on her answering machine was flashing. It would take too long to put on her slippers, so she walked across the cold floor, her toes curling with each step. Her walking partner, Amy, was standing outside the door.

'You stood me up again," she said as she pushed herself in. Sunny was lucky to have a walking partner; it was someone who would miss her. Close relations were relative here at Regal Crest. Even though Sunny belonged to many clubs, she wouldn't necessarily go missing.

"Do you even remember how cold it is by the bench?" Amy smiled and made her way over to the kitchen table. It had been Sunny's idea when renovating that she wanted a kitchen that would be welcoming, where people could just drop by. And it worked.

Amy dropped her house keys, her cell phone and water bottle on the table, but then picked up the water bottle again, checked the water level and went over to the faucet. "Keeping hydrated is not easy to do and you have to pee all the time. I'm not ready for pee pads yet. Do you remember when we went to that Motown concert in the Clubhouse Auditorium? It was a long time to intermission. When the lights went on, I jumped up and made my way up the aisle to get to the bathroom before the line at the ladies room formed. But there was no one waiting. And it occurred to me, like a bolt of lightning, that everyone was wearing Depends and happily sitting in their pee. Yuck! That will never be me. You think I dropped by to visit you? Well, it was actually to use your facilities." Amy laughed and made her way over to the guest bathroom.

*It was ridiculous having the bathroom so close to the living area and kitchen. You could hear everything,* Sunny thought as the toilet flushed. She'd have to do something about that one day.

*SUNFLOWER*

# Chapter 48

# Sunny: Two Years Later

SUNNY'S EYES POPPED open as they did every day. She wasn't one to have a slow entry from sleep to awake, and her mind immediately started clicking with her plans and problem-solving for the day. When her mind got so full that she couldn't keep track of it all, she would roll over, reach for her notebook, and hope she could capture her thoughts and ideas on paper. And recently, the length of her capacity seemed to be getting shorter and shorter.

It was hard to believe two years had passed. The movie theater was still going strong with good attendance. It was a good addition to the community. Many of the larger condos had their own movie screenings in their party rooms, the church had spiritual screenings and there were a couple of movie clubs focusing on oldies but goodies. Nevertheless, there was something to be said for the big screen, the soft seats and all the perks that came with an actual movie theater. And the films had been "old people" specific.

In fact, last night, she went to a screening of *Still Alice*, which is about a woman with early onset Alzheimer's. Julianne Moore had won the Academy Award for Best Actress, and she deserved it. But it was very hard to watch, and Sunny went from squirming in her chair to being on the brink of tears through much of the film. It was true they were showing more films about older people as the population aged, but perhaps something more upbeat would be better. As Alice experienced memory lapses, Sunny could only think about when similar episodes had happened to her. For example, she had the floor presenting an argument for a controversial point at the book club when all of a sudden, her mind went blank. As hard as she tried, she couldn't retrieve even a thread of what she was saying; and the harder she tried, the emptier her mind became except for an overwhelming sweep of embarrassment. She looked around and only sensed pity from the other members. Finally, she had to give up the floor. As soon as she did that, the memories came flooding back, but by then the conversation had swung to different issues.

Sure, she hadn't lost her way (yet) when she was out and about, but she had placed her keys in a weird location on more than one occasion. But then she and three friends were discussing sixties music, and no one could come up with the name of the drummer for the Beatles, so maybe it was inevitable and happened to everyone when they aged.

Sunny got up and shuffled to the kitchen to start the coffeemaker. She looked at the calendar on her kitchen wall, as she did every day. Yes, it was hard to believe that almost two years had passed since the incident at the theater and all that it encompassed had happened. She would be 70 years old in a couple of days, and if plans had been in place... She shuddered to think of what it would mean. But sometimes, she wondered.

Maybe there's a phase in your life wherein more people, friends and acquaintances die. Recently, there seemed to be more notices than she remembered in the *Regal Crest News*. In her building's lobby, two plastic frames were simultaneously displayed with information about two upcoming funerals. At the monthly Travel Club meeting, it was announced that Mark and Elizabeth, husband and wife, had died within two months of each other, although they appeared to be healthy and aging gracefully.

There was only one way to answer that question. For the past two years—for the past 730 days—each day began with the resolve that today, she would do something, but then it was left as a tiny burning sensation at the back of Sunny's mind, neglected as she went about her day. It was easier to try to pretend that it never happened. In fact, as it got further and further away, the more unreal it became.

In the beginning, she thought she might be able to share what she thought she knew with someone. But it seemed so farfetched and silly. Who would believe her, especially now? It was a hard secret to keep, but even a harder secret to tell.

This morning, she was going to a meeting of the Politics Club, where she was in charge of the postcard campaign—sending short missives to county leaders about the needs of Regal Crest residents—specifically a change in the bus route so that it would make a stop at Regal Crest on its way to the medical complex a few miles outside the gate. She tried to keep up with the news, but on this day in particular, she made sure to watch CNN and read the local newspaper so she would be up to date with what was happening in the community and the wider political world. It would be sure to come up at the meeting.

An hour later, she was running out the door, late as usual. It's a good thing the Clubhouse was only two blocks away. She let the door slam behind her as she rushed down the hall. She had no double locks or safety chains. Living at Regal Crest felt safe.

Don, the mailman, was finishing filling the boxes in the lobby. "Hi, Mrs. Meyers. Looks like I have one of these letters for you. I've been delivering a lot of these lately." He handed Sunny a cream envelope with gold lettering, and looked as if he was hoping Sunny would open the envelope now so he could see what it was.

*He'll just have to wonder. I can't be later than I am.* Sunny took the envelope out of Don's hand and glanced at the return address, "E-PEP @ Regal Crest", before stuffing it in her handbag. *That acronym sounds familiar*, she thought. *I'll read it later.*

# Acknowledgments

WRITING HAS BEEN an avocation and an integral part of my life for as long as I can remember. But it wasn't until I joined the Writers' Group of my new retirement community that I developed a regular writing practice. It was a great motivator knowing that I would need something fresh to share at the next meeting and being part of a group of dedicated writers was inspirational. Thank you, fellow writers.

Thanks especially to York Van Nixon III, a prolific writer who is my mentor and role model. York invited me to join his novel writing group, "Thoth Fingers". It was while I was attending those weekly meetings that I started and developed "Shadow of Youth", one chapter at a time. Thanks also to Tom Anessi, the remaining member of this novel group, for his comments on the early chapters I shared with participants.

I am fortunate to have the support and encouragement of my family and friends in this endeavor. A special thanks to my "readers" who helped edit my drafts, gave detailed recommendations, reminded me that "You can do it!", and kept me to task when I got cold feet. They are Harry Denny, Betsy Haas, Kathleen Hamill, Kay Haskins, Bari Haskins-Jackson, Glenne Martin and Helen Mays.

Made in the USA
Columbia, SC
22 July 2019